DAUBER
& REYNARD THE FOX

TWO TALES IN VERSE

Dauber
& Reynard the Fox

JOHN MASEFIELD

THE MACMILLAN COMPANY
NEW YORK

Printed in Great Britain by Morrison and Gibb Ltd.
London and Edinburgh

Contents

29955

Dauber

INTRODUCTION

THE STORY *Dauber* was written during the spring, summer and autumn of 1912, in London and at Great Hampden in Buckinghamshire.

It is the story of a young man who wished to paint ships and the sea, and therefore shipped himself to sea that he might know these, and perhaps in a few long voyages, earn enough money to pay for training in an art-school. This was the law of his being; he obeyed it, as men will, whatever the cost in suffering to himself. He had a determination which carried him through the beginnings of the struggle with credit.

After some time at sea, while he was serving in a barque in the South Pacific, he fell from aloft and was killed as I have told. One of his shipmates described the case to me, thus:

I was below, in the half-deck, with the others of my watch, when we heard the royals coming in, and soon afterwards the topgallants being let-go and clewd-up. A minute or two later, as we sat wondering if we

should be called on deck to shorten sail, I heard a
queer kind of thud from somewhere forward, and
asked: 'What was that noise?'

Someone said, 'Only a coil of rope being flung
down.'

I said, 'It didn't sound to me quite like a coil of
rope.' A minute later I heard the Captain, aft on the
poop, crying out to the officer of the watch (who
was forward somewhere) that there was a man of his
watch lying on the deck. At that, I jumped up, grabbed
a bucket with some fresh water in it, and ran on deck.
I found Dauber lying on the deck forward, at the
point of death. He said 'It will go on,' and died, just
as I reached him. It was very sad for all of us.

He had gone up with another couple of men to
stow the fore topgallant sail and in a gust the sail
flung up and knocked him from the yard: the man
next to him almost came with him.

The wind was little more than a squall: we soon
had the royals set again, but in the dark that night,
I had to go up to the fore topgallant yard, to the very
place from which he fell, and while I was there, the
over-hauled royal buntline came ever so gently over
my head, like somebody stroking me, and I was so
scared that I as nearly as possible fell, too.

In those days, in the late nineteenth century, few
youths had the courage to give up every known ease of
life for the sake, or in the hope, of one of the arts. Today,
it may be that there are even fewer such. To myself

Dauber remains an image of one who knows the law of his being, and obeys that law, cost what it may, through misery to early death if necessary. If the star in the mind shine bright, what does other darkness matter?

JOHN MASEFIELD

I

FOUR bells were struck, the watch was called on deck
All work aboard was over for the hour,
And some men sang and others played at check,
Or mended clothes or watched the sunset glower.
The bursting west was like an opening flower,
And one man watched it till the light was dim,
But no one went across to talk to him.

He was the painter in that swift's ship crew—
Lampman and painter—tall, a slight-built man,
Young for his years, and not yet twenty-two;
Sickly, and not yet brown with the sea's tan.
Bullied and damned at since the voyage began,
'Being neither man nor seaman by his tally,'
He bunked with the idlers just abaft the galley.

His work began at five; he worked all day,
Keeping no watch and having all night in.
His work was what the mate might care to say;
He mixed red lead in many a bouilli tin;
His dungarees were smeared with paraffin.
'Go drown himself' his round-house mates advised him,
And all hands called him 'Dauber' and despised him.

4

Si, the apprentice, stood beside the spar,
Stripped to the waist, a basin at his side,
Slushing his hands to get away the tar,
And then he washed himself and rinsed and dried;
Towelling his face, hair-towzelled, eager-eyed,
He crossed the spar to Dauber, and there stood
Watching the gold of heaven turn to blood.

They stood there by the rail while the swift ship
Tore on out of the tropics, straining her sheets,
Whitening her trackway to a milky strip,
Dim with green bubbles and twisted water-meets,
Her clacking tackle tugged at pins and cleats,
Her great sails bellied stiff, her great masts leaned:
They watched how the seas struck and burst and greened.

Si talked with Dauber, standing by the side.
'Why did you come to sea, painter?' he said.
'I want to be a painter,' he replied,
'And know the sea and ships from A to Z,
And paint great ships at sea before I'm dead;
Ships under skysails running down the Trade—
Ships and the sea; there's nothing finer made.

'But there's so much to learn, with sails and ropes,
And how the sails look, full or being furled,
And how the lights change in the troughs and slopes,
And the sea's colours up and down the world,
And how a storm looks when the sprays are hurled
High as the yard (they say) I want to see;
There's none ashore can teach such things to me.

'And then the men and rigging, and the way
Ships move, running or beating, and the poise
At the roll's end, the checking in the sway—
I want to paint them perfect, short of the noise;
And then the life, the half-decks full of boys,
The fo'c's'les with the men there, dripping wet.
I know the subjects that I want to get.

'It's not been done, the sea, not yet been done,
From the inside, by one who really knows;
I'd give up all if I could be the one,
But art comes dear the way the money goes.
So I have come to sea, and I suppose
Three years will teach me all I want to learn
And make enough to keep me till I earn.'

Even as he spoke his busy pencil moved,
Drawing the leap of water off the side
Where the great clipper trampled iron-hooved.
Making the blue hills of the sea divide,
Shearing a glittering scatter in her stride,
And leaping on full tilt with all sails drawing,
Proud as a war-horse, snuffing battle, pawing.

'I cannot get it yet—not yet,' he said;
'That leap and light, and sudden change to green,
And all the glittering from the sunset's red,
And the milky colours where the bursts have been,
And then the clipper striding like a queen
Over it all, all beauty to the crown.
I see it all, I cannot put it down.

'It's hard not to be able. There, look there!
I cannot get the movement nor the light;
Sometimes it almost makes a man despair
To try and try and never get it right.
Oh, if I could—oh, if I only might,
I wouldn't mind what hells I'd have to pass,
Not if the whole world called me fool and ass.'

Down sank the crimson sun into the sea,
The wind cut chill at once, the west grew dun.
'Out sidelights!' called the mate. 'Hi, where is he?'
The Boatswain called, 'Out sidelights, damn you! Run!'
'He's always late or lazing,' murmured one—
'The Dauber, with his sketching.' Soon the tints
Of red and green passed on dark water-glints.

Darker it grew, still darker, and the stars
Burned golden, and the fiery fishes came.
The wire-note loudened from the straining spars;
The sheet-blocks clacked together always the same;
The rushing fishes streaked the seas with flame,
Racing the one speed noble as their own:
What unknown joy was in those fish unknown!

Just by the round-house door, as it grew dark,
The Boatswain caught the Dauber with, 'Now, you;
Till now I've spared you, damn you! now you hark:
I've just had hell for what you didn't do;
I'll have you broke and sent among the crew
If you get me more trouble by a particle.
Don't you forget, you daubing, useless article!

'You thing, you twice-laid thing from Port Mahon!'
Then came the Cook's 'Is that the Dauber there?
Why don't you leave them stinking paints alone?
They stink the house out, poisoning all the air.
Just take them out.' 'Where to?' 'I don't care where.
I won't have stinking paint here.' From their plates:
'That's right; wet paint breeds fever,' growled his mates.

He took his still wet drawings from the berth
And climbed the ladder to the deck-house top;
Beneath, the noisy half-deck rang with mirth,
For two ship's boys were putting on the strop;
One, clambering up to let the skylight drop,
Saw him bend down beneath a boat and lay
His drawings there, till all were hid away.

And stand there silent, leaning on the boat,
Watching the constellations rise and burn,
Until the beauty took him by the throat,
So stately is their glittering overturn;
Armies of marching eyes, armies that yearn
With banners rising and falling, and passing by
Over the empty silence of the sky.

The Dauber sighed there looking at the sails,
Wind-steadied arches leaning on the night,
The high trucks traced on heaven and left no trails;
The moonlight made the topsails almost white,
The passing sidelight seemed to drip green light.
And on the clipper rushed with fire-bright bows;
He sighed, 'I'll never do 't,' and left the house.

'Now,' said the reefer, 'Up! Come, Sam; come, Si,
Dauber's been hiding something.' Up they slid,
Treading on naked tiptoe stealthily
To grope for treasure at the long-boat skid.
'Drawings!' said Sam. 'Is that what Dauber hid?
Lord! I expected pudding, not this rot.
Still, come, we'll have some fun with what we've got.'

They smeared the paint with turpentine until
They could remove with mess-clouts every trace
Of quick perception caught by patient skill,
And lines that had brought blood into his face.
They wiped the pigments off, and did erase,
With knives, all sticking clots. When they had done,
Under the boat they laid them every one.

All he had drawn since first he came to sea,
His six weeks' leisure's fruits, they laid them there.
They chuckled then to think how mad he'd be
Finding his paintings vanished into air.
Eight bells were struck, and feet from everywhere
Went shuffling aft to muster in the dark;
The mate's pipe glowed above, a dim red spark.

Names in the darkness passed and voices cried;
The red spark glowed and died, the faces seemed
As things remembered when a brain has died,
To all but high intenseness deeply dreamed.
Like hissing spears the fishes' fire streamed,
And on the clipper rushed with tossing mast,
A bath of flame broke round her as she passed.

The watch was set, the night came, and the men
Hid from the moon in shadowed nooks to sleep,
Bunched like the dead; still, like the dead, as when
Plague in a city leaves none even to weep.
The ship's track brightened to a mile-broad sweep;
The mate there felt her pulse, and eyed the spars;
South-west by south she staggered under the stars

Down in his bunk the Dauber lay awake
Thinking of his unfitness for the sea.
Each failure, each derision, each mistake,
There in the life not made for such as he;
A morning grim with trouble sure to be,
A noon of pain from failure, and a night
Bitter with men's contemning and despite.

This is the first beginning, the green leaf,
Still in the Trades before bad weather fell;
What harvest would he reap of hate and grief
When the loud Horn made every life a hell?
When the sick ship lay over, clanging her bell,
And no time came for painting or for drawing,
But all hands fought, and icy death came clawing?

Hell, he expected,—hell. His eyes grew blind;
The snoring from his messmates droned and snuffled,
And then a gush of pity calmed his mind.
The cruel torment of his thought was muffled,
Without, on deck, an old, old seaman shuffled,
Humming his song, and through the open door
A moonbeam moved and thrust along the floor.

The green bunk curtains moved, the brass rings clicked,
The Cook cursed in his sleep, turning and turning,
The moonbeam's moving finger touched and picked,
And all the stars in all the sky were burning.
'This is the art I've come for, and am learning,
The sea and ships and men and travelling things.
It is most proud, whatever pain it brings.'

He leaned upon his arm and watched the light
Sliding and fading to the steady roll;
This he would some day paint, the ship at night
And sleeping seamen tired to the soul;
The space below the bunks as black as coal,
Gleams upon chests, upon the unlit lamp,
The ranging door-hook, and the locker clamp.

This he would paint, and that, and all these scenes,
And proud ships carrying on, and men their minds,
And blues of rollers toppling into greens,
And shattering into white that bursts and blinds,
And scattering ships running erect like hinds,
And men in oilskins beating down a sail
High on the yellow yard, in snow, in hail.

With faces ducked down from the slanting drive
Of half-thawed hail mixed with half-frozen spray,
The roaring canvas, like a thing alive,
Shaking the mast, knocking their hands away
The foot-ropes jerking to the tug and sway,
The savage eyes salt-reddened at the rims,
And icicles on the south-wester brims.

D.—2

And sunnier scenes would grow under his brush,
The tropic dawn with all things dropping dew,
The darkness and the wonder and the hush,
The insensate grey before the marvel grew;
Then the veil lifted from the trembling blue,
The walls of sky burst in, the flower, the rose,
All the expanse of heaven a mind that glows.

He turned out of his bunk; the Cook still tossed,
One of the other two spoke in his sleep,
A cockroach scuttled where the moonbeam crossed;
Outside there was the ship, the night, the deep.
'It is worth while,' the youth said; 'I will keep
To my resolve, I'll learn to paint all this.
My Lord, my God, how beautiful it is!'

Outside was the ship's rush to the wind's hurry
A resonant wire-hum from every rope,
The broadening bow-wash in a fiery flurry,
The leaning masts in their majestic slope,
And all things strange with moonlight: filled with hope
By all that beauty going as man bade,
He turned and slept in peace. Eight bells were made.

II

Next day was Sunday, his free painting day,
While the fine weather held, from eight till eight.
He rose when called at five, and did array
The round-house gear, and set the kit-bags straight
Then kneeling down, like housemaid at a grate,
He scrubbed the deck with sand until his knees
Were blue with dye from his wet dungarees.

Soon all was clean, his Sunday tasks were done;
His day was clear for painting as he chose.
The wetted decks were drying in the sun,
The men coiled up, or swabbed, or sought repose.
The drifts of silver arrows fell and rose
As flying fish took wing; the breakfast passed,
Wasting good time, but he was free at last.

Free for two hours and more to tingle deep,
Catching a likeness in a line or tint,
The canvas running up in a proud sweep,
Wind-wrinkled at the clews, and white like lint,
The glittering of the blue waves into glint;
Free to attempt it all, the proud ship's pawings.
The sea, the sky—he went to fetch his drawings.

Up to the deck-house top he quickly climbed,
He stooped to find them underneath the boat.
He found them all obliterated, slimed,
Blotted, erased, gone from him line and note.
They were all spoiled: a lump came in his throat,
Being vain of his attempts, and tender skinned—
Beneath the skylight watching reefers grinned.

He clambered down, holding the ruined things.
'Bosun,' he called, 'look here, did you do these:
Wipe off my paints and cut them into strings,
And smear them till you can't tell chalk from cheese?
Don't stare, but did you do it? Answer, please.'
The Bosun turned: 'I'll give you a thick ear!
Do it? I didn't. Get to hell from here!

'I touch your stinking daubs? The Dauber's daft.'
A crowd was gathering now to hear the fun;
The reefers tumbled out, the men laid aft,
The Cook blinked, cleaning a mess-kid in the sun.
'What's up with Dauber now?' said everyone.
'Someone has spoiled my drawings—look at this!'
'Well, that's a dirty trick, by God, it is!'

'It is,' said Sam, 'a low-down dirty trick,
To spoil a fellow's work in such a way,
And if you catch him, Dauber, punch him sick,
For he deserves it, be he who he may.'
A seaman shook his old head wise and grey.
'It seems to me,' he said, 'who ain't no judge,
Then drawings look much better now they're smudge.'

'Where were they, Dauber? On the deck-house? Where?'
'Under the long-boat, in a secret place.'
'The blackguard must have seen you put them there.
He is a swine! I tell him to his face:
I didn't think we'd anyone so base.'
'Nor I,' said Dauber. 'There was six weeks' time
Just wasted in these drawings: it's a crime!'

'Well, don't you say we did it,' growled his mates,
'And as for crime, be damned! the things were smears—
Best overboard, like you, with shot for weights;
Thank God they're gone, and now go shake your ears.'
The Dauber listened, very near to tears.
'Dauber, if I were you,' said Sam again,
'I'd aft, and see the Captain and complain.'

A sigh came from the assembled seamen there.
Would he be such a fool for their delight
As go to tell the Captain? Would he dare?
And would the thunder roar, the lightning smite?
There was the Captain come to take a sight,
Handling his sextant by the chart-house aft.
The Dauber turned, the seamen thought him daft.

The Captain took his sights—a mate below
Noted the times; they shouted to each other,
The Captain quick with 'Stop,' the answer slow,
Repeating slowly one height then another.
The swooping clipper stumbled through the smother,
The ladder brasses in the sunlight burned,
The Dauber waited till the Captain turned.

There stood the Dauber, humbled to the bone,
Waiting to speak. The Captain let him wait,
Glanced at the course, and called in even tone,
'What is the man there wanting, Mr Mate?'
The logship clattered on the grating straight,
The reel rolled to the scuppers with a clatter,
The Mate came grim: 'Well, Dauber, what's the matter?'

'Please sir, they spoiled my drawings.' 'Who did?' 'They.'
'Who's they?' 'I don't quite know, sir.' 'Don't quite know,
    sir?
Then why are you aft to talk about it, hey?
Whom d'you complain of?' 'No one.' 'No one?' 'No, sir.'
'Well, then, go forward till you've found them. Go, sir.
If you complain of someone, then I'll see.
Now get to hell! and don't come bothering me.'

'But, sir, they washed them off, and some they cut.
Look here, sir, how they spoiled them.' 'Never mind.
Go shove your head inside the scuttle butt,
And that will make you cooler. You will find
Nothing like water when you're mad and blind.
Where were the drawings? in your chest, or where?'
'Under the long-boat, sir; I put them there.'

'Under the long-boat, hey? Now mind your tip.
I'll have the skids kept clear with nothing round them;
The long-boat ain't a store in this here ship.
Lucky for you it wasn't I who found them.
If I had seen them, Dauber, I'd have drowned them.
Now you be warned by this. I tell you plain—
Don't stow your brass-rags under boats again.

'Go forward to your berth.' The Dauber turned.
The listeners down below them winked and smiled,
Knowing how red the Dauber's temples burned,
Having lost the case about his only child.
His work was done to nothing and defiled,
And there was no redress: the Captain's voice
Spoke, and called, 'Painter', making him rejoice.

The Captain and the Mate conversed together.
'Drawings, you tell me, Mister?' 'Yes, sir; views
Wiped off with turps, I gather that's his blether.
He says they're things he can't afford to lose.
He's Dick, who came to sea in dancing shoes,
And found the dance a bear dance. They were hidden
Under the long-boat's chocks, which I've forbidden."

'Wiped off with turps?' The Captain sucked his lip
'Who did it, Mister?' 'Reefers, I suppose;
Them devils do the most pranks in a ship;
The round-house might have done it, Cook or Bose.'
'I can't take notice of it till he knows.
How does he do his work?' 'Well, no offence;
He tries; he does his best. He's got no sense.'

'Painter,' the Captain called; the Dauber came.
'What's all this talk of drawings? What's the matter?'
'They spoiled my drawings, sir.' 'Well, who's to blame?
The long-boat's there for no one to get at her;
You broke the rules, and if you choose to scatter
Gear up and down where it's no right to be,
And suffer as result, don't come to me.

'Your place is in the round-house, and your gear
Belongs where you belong. Who spoiled your things?
Find out who spoiled your things and fetch him here.'
'But, sir, they cut the canvas into strings.'
'I want no argument nor questionings.
Go back where you belong and say no more,
And please remember that you're not on shore.'

The Dauber touched his brow and slunk away—
They eyed his going with a bitter eye.
'Dauber,' said Sam, 'what did the Captain say?'
The Dauber drooped his head without reply.
'Go forward, Dauber, and enjoy your cry.'
The Mate limped to the rail; like little feet
Over his head the drumming reef-points beat.

The Dauber reached the berth and entered in.
Much mockery followed after as he went,
And each face seemed to greet him with the grin
Of hounds hot following on a creature spent.
'Aren't you a fool?' each mocking visage meant.
'Who did it, Dauber? What did Captain say?
It is a crime, and there'll be hell to pay.'

He bowed his head, the house was full of smoke;
The Sails was pointing shackles on his chest.
'Lord, Dauber, be a man and take a joke'—
He puffed his pipe—'and let the matter rest.
Spit brown, my son, and get a hairy breast;
Get shoulders on you at the crojick braces,
And let this painting business go to blazes.

'What good can painting do to anyone?
I don't say never do it; far from that—
No harm in sometimes painting just for fun.
Keep it for fun, and stick to what you're at.
Your job's to fill your bones up and get fat;
Rib up like Barney's Bull, and thick your neck.
Throw paints to hell, boy; you belong on deck.'

'That's right,' said Chips; 'it's downright good advice.
Painting's no good; what good can painting do
Up on a lower topsail stiff with ice,
With all your little fish-hooks frozen blue?
Painting won't help you at the weather clew,
Nor pass your gaskets for you, nor make sail.
Painting's a balmy job not worth a nail.'

The Dauber did not answer; time was passing.
He pulled his easel out, his paints, his stool.
The wind was dropping, and the sea was glassing—
New realms of beauty waited for his rule;
The draught out of the crojick kept him cool.
He sat to paint, alone and melancholy.
'No turning fools,' the Chips said, 'from their folly.'

He dipped his brush and tried to fix a line,
And then came peace, and gentle beauty came,
Turning his spirit's water into wine,
Lightening his darkness with a touch of flame.
O, joy of trying for beauty, ever the same,
You never fail, your comforts never end;
O, balm of this world's way; O, perfect friend!

III

THEY lost the Trades soon after; then came calm,
Light little gusts and rain, which soon increased
To glorious northers shouting out a psalm
At seeing the bright blue water silver fleeced;
Hornwards she rushed, trampling the seas to yeast.
There fell a rain-squall in a blind day's end
When for an hour the Dauber found a friend.

Out of the rain the voices called and passed,
The staysails flogged, the tackle yanked and shook.
Inside the harness-room a lantern cast
Light and wild shadows as it ranged its hook.
The watch on deck was gathered in the nook,
They had taken shelter in that secret place,
Wild light gave wild emotions to each face.

One beat the beef-cask, and the others sang
A song that had brought anchors out of seas
In ports where bells of Christians never rang,
Nor any sea mark blazed among the trees.
By forlorn swamps, in ice, by windy keys,
That song had sounded; now it shook the air
From these eight wanderers brought together there.

Under the poop-break, sheltering from the rain,
The Dauber sketched some likeness of the room,
A note to be a prompting to his brain,
A spark to make old memory reillume.
'Dauber,' said someone near him in the gloom,
'How goes it, Dauber?' It was reefer Si.
'There's not much use in trying to keep dry.'

They sat upon the sail-room doorway coaming,
The lad held forth like youth, the Dauber listened
To how the boy had had a taste for roaming,
And what the sea is said to be and isn't.
Where the dim lamplight fell the wet deck glistened,
Si said the Horn was still some weeks away,
'But tell me, Dauber, where d'you hail from? Eh?'

The rain blew past and let the stars appear;
The seas grew larger as the moonlight grew
For half an hour the ring of heaven was clear,
Dusty with moonlight, grey rather than blue;
In that great moon the showing stars were few.
The sleepy time-boy's feet passed overhead.
'I come from out past Gloucester,' Dauber said;

'Not far from Pauntley, if you know those parts;
The place is Spital Farm, near Silver Hill,
Above a trap-hatch where a mill-stream starts.
We had a mill once, but we've stopped the mill,
My dad and sister keep the farm on still.
We're only tenants, but we've rented there,
Father and son, for over eighty year.

'Father has worked the farm since grandfer went;
It means the world to him; I can't think why
They bleed him to the last half-crown for rent,
And this and that have almost milked him dry.
The land's all starved; if he'd put money by,
And corn was up, and rent was down two-thirds. . . .
But then they aren't, so what's the use of words.

'Yet still he couldn't bear to see it pass
To strangers, or to think a time would come
When other men than us would mow the grass,
And other names than ours have the home.
Some sorrows come from evil thought, but some
Comes when two men are near, and both are blind
To what is generous in the other's mind.

'I was the only boy, and father thought
I'd farm the Spital after he was dead,
And many a time he took me out and taught
About manures and seed-corn white and red,
And soils and hops, but I'd an empty head;
Harvest or seed, I would not do a turn—
I loathed the farm, I didn't want to learn.

'He did not mind at first, he thought it youth
Feeling the collar, and that I should change.
Then time gave him some inklings of the truth,
And that I loathed the farm, and wished to range.
Truth to a man of fifty's always strange;
It was most strange and terrible to him
That I, his heir, should be the devil's limb.

'Yet still he hoped the Lord might change my mind.
I'd see him bridle in his wrath and hate,
And almost break my heart he was so kind,
Biting his lips sore with resolve to wait.
And then I'd try awhile; but it was Fate:
I didn't want to learn; the farm to me
Was mire and hopeless work and misery.

'Though there were things I loved about it, too—
The beasts, the apple-trees, and going haying.
And then I tried; but no, it wouldn't do,
The farm was prison, and my thoughts were straying.
And there'd come father, with his grey head, praying,
"O, my dear son, don't let the Spital pass;
It's my old home, boy, where your grandfer was.

' "And now you won't learn farming; you don't care,
The old home's nought to you. I've tried to teach you;
I've begged Almighty God, boy, all I dare,
To use His hand if word of mine won't reach you.
Boy, for your grandfer's sake I do beseech you,
Don't let the Spital pass to strangers. Squire
Has said he'd give it you if we require.

' "Your mother used to walk here, boy, with me,
It was her favourite walk down to the mill;
And there we'd talk how little death would be,
Knowing our work was going on here still.
You've got the brains, you only want the will—
Don't disappoint your mother and your father.
I'll give you time to travel, if you'd rather."

'But, no, I'd wander up the brooks to read.
Then sister Jane would start with nagging tongue,
Saying my sin made father's heart to bleed,
And how she feared she'd live to see me hung.
And then she'd read me bits from Dr Young.
And when we three would sit to supper, Jane
Would fillip dad till dad began again.

' "I've been here all my life, boy. I was born
Up in the room above—looks on the mead.
I never thought you'd cockle my clean corn,
And leave the old home to a stranger's seed.
Father and I have made here 'thout a weed:
We've give our lives to make that. Eighty years.
And now I go down to the grave in tears."

'And then I'd get ashamed and take off coat,
And work maybe a week, ploughing and sowing,
And then I'd creep away and sail my boat,
Or watch the water when the mill was going.
That's my delight—to be near water flowing,
Dabbling or sailing boats or jumping stanks,
Or finding moorhens' nests along the banks.

'And one day father found a ship I'd built;
He took the cart-whip to me over that,
And I, half mad with pain, and sick with guilt,
Went up and hid in what we called the flat,
A dusty hole given over to the cat.
She kittened there; the kittens had worn paths
Among the cobwebs, dust, and broken laths.

'And putting down my hand between the beams
I felt a leathery thing, and pulled it clear:
A book with white cocoons stuck in the seams,
Where spiders had had nests for many a year.
It was my mother's sketch-book; hid, I fear,
Lest dad should ever see it. Mother's life
Was not her own while she was father's wife.

'There were her drawings, dated, pencilled faint.
March was the last one, eighteen eighty-three,
Unfinished that, for tears had smeared the paint.
The rest was landscape, not yet brought to be.
That was a holy afternoon to me;
That book a sacred book; the flat a place
Where I could meet my mother face to face.

'She had found peace of spirit, mother had,
Drawing the landscape from the attic there—
Heart-broken, often, after rows with dad,
Hid like a wild thing in a secret lair.
That rotting sketch-book showed me how and where
I, too, could get away; and then I knew
That drawing was the work I longed to do.

'Drawing became my life. I drew, I toiled,
And every penny I could get I spent
On paints and artist's matters, which I spoiled
Up in the attic to my heart's content,
Till one day father asked me what I meant;
The time had come, he said, to make an end.
Now it must finish: what did I intend?

'Either I took to farming, like his son,
In which case he would teach me, early and late
(Provided that my daubing mood was done),
Or I must go; it must be settled straight.
If I refused to farm, there was the gate.
I was to choose, his patience was all gone,
The present state of things could not go on.

'Sister was there; she eyed me while he spoke.
The kitchen clock ran down and struck the hour,
And something told me father's heart was broke,
For all he stood so set and looked so sour.
Jane took a duster, and began to scour
A pewter on the dresser; she was crying.
I stood stock still a long time, not replying.

'Dad waited, then he snorted and turned round.
"Well, think of it," he said. He left the room,
His boots went clop along the stony ground
Out to the orchard and the apple-bloom.
A cloud came past the sun and made a gloom;
I swallowed with dry lips, then sister turned.
She was dead white but for her eyes that burned.

' "You're breaking father's heart, Joe," she began;
"It's not as if—" she checked, in too much pain.
"O, Joe, don't help to kill so fine a man;
You're giving him our mother over again.
It's wearing him to death, Joe, heart and brain;
You know what store he sets on leaving this
To (it's too cruel) to a son of his.

' "Yet you go painting all the day. O Joe,
Couldn't you make an effort? Can't you see
What folly it is of yours? It's not as though
You are a genius, or could ever be.
O Joe, for father's sake, if not for me,
Give up this craze for painting, and be wise
And work with father, where your duty lies."

' "It goes too deep," I said; "I loathe the farm;
I couldn't help, even if I'd the mind.
Even if I helped, I'd only do him harm;
Father would see it, if he were not blind.
I was not built to farm, as he would find.
O Jane, it's bitter hard to stand alone
And spoil my father's life or spoil my own."

' "Spoil both," she said, "the way you're shaping now.
You're only a boy not knowing your own good.
Where will you go, suppose you leave here? How
Do you propose to earn your daily food?
Draw? Daub the pavements? There's a feckless brood
Goes to the devil daily, Joe, in cities
Only from thinking how divine their wit is.

' "Clouds are they, without water, carried away.
And you'll be one of them, the way you're going,
Daubing at silly pictures all the day,
And praised by silly fools who're always blowing.
And you chose this when you might go a-sowing,
Casting the good corn into chosen mould
That shall in time bring forth a hundredfold."

D.—3

'So we went on, but in the end it ended.
I felt I'd done a murder; I felt sick.
There's much in human minds cannot be mended,
And that, not I, played dad a cruel trick.
There was one mercy: that it ended quick.
I went to join my mother's brother: he
Lived down the Severn. He was kind to me.

'And there I learned house-painting for a living.
I'd have been happy there, but that I knew
I'd sinned before my father past forgiving,
And that they sat at home, that silent two,
Wearing the fire out and the evening through,
Silent, defeated, broken, in despair,
My plate unset, my name gone, and my chair.

'I saw all that; and sister Jane came white—
White as a ghost, with fiery, weeping eyes.
I saw her all day long and half the night,
Bitter as gall, and passionate and wise.
"Joe, you have killed your father: there he lies.
You have done your work—you with our mother's ways."
She said it plain, and then her eyes would blaze.

'And then one day I had a job to do
Down below bridge, by where the docks begin,
And there I saw a clipper towing through,
Up from the sea that morning, entering in.
Raked to the nines she was, lofty and thin,
Her ensign ruffling red, her bunts in pile,
Beauty and strength together, wonder, style.

'She docked close to the gates, and there she lay
Over the water from me, well in sight;
And as I worked I watched her all the day,
Finding her beauty ever fresh delight.
Her house-flag was bright green with strips of white;
High in the sunny air it rose to shake
Above the skysail poles most splendid rake.

'And when I felt unhappy I would look
Over the river at her, and her pride,
So calm, so quiet, came as a rebuke
To half the passionate pathways which I tried;
And though the autumn ran its term and died,
And winter fell and cold December came,
She was still splendid there, and still the same.

'Then on a day she sailed; but when she went
My mind was clear on what I had to try:
To see the sea and ships, and what they meant,
That was the thing I longed to do; so I
Drew and worked hard, and studied and put by,
And thought of nothing else but that one end,
But let all else go hang—love, money, friend.

'And now I've shipped as Dauber I've begun.
It was hard work to find a dauber's berth;
I hadn't any friends to find me one,
Only my skill, for what it may be worth;
But I'm at sea now, going about the earth,
And when the ship's paid off, when we return,
I'll join some Paris studio and learn.'

He stopped, the air came moist, Si did not speak;
The Dauber turned his eyes to where he sat,
Pressing the sail-room hinges with his cheek,
His face half covered with a drooping hat.
Huge dewdrops from the staysails dropped and spat,
Si did not stir, the Dauber touched his sleeve,
A little birdlike noise came from a sheave.

Si was asleep, sleeping a calm deep sleep,
Still as a warden of the Egyptian dead
In some old haunted temple buried deep
Under the desert sand, sterile and red.
The Dauber shook his arm; Si jumped and said,
'Good yarn, I swear! I say, you have a brain—
Was that eight bells that went?' He slept again.

Then waking up, 'I've had a nap,' he cried.
'Was that one bell? What, Dauber, you still here?'
'Si there?' the Mate's voice called. 'Sir,' he replied.
The order made the lad's thick vision clear;
A something in the Mate's voice made him fear
'Si,' said the Mate, 'I hear you've made a friend—
Dauber, in short. That friendship's got to end.

'You're a young gentleman. Your place aboard
Is with the gentlemen abaft the mast.
You're learning to command; you can't afford
To yarn with any man. But there . . . it's past.
You've done it once; let this time be the last.
The Dauber's place is forward. Do it again,
I'll put you bunking forward with the men.

'Dismiss.' Si went, but Sam, beside the Mate,
Timekeeper there, walked with him to the rail
And whispered him the menace of 'You wait'—
Words which have turned full many a reefer pale.
The watch was changed; the watch on deck trimmed sail.
Sam, going below, called all the reefers down,
Sat in his bunk and eyed them with a frown.

'Si here,' he said, 'has soiled the half-deck's name
Talking to Dauber—Dauber, the ship's clout.
A reefer takes the Dauber for a flame,
The half-deck take the round-house walking out.
He's soiled the half-deck's honour; now, no doubt,
The Bosun and his mates will come here sneaking,
Asking for smokes, or blocking gangways speaking.

'I'm not a vain man, given to blow or boast;
I'm not a proud man, but I truly feel
That while I've bossed this mess and ruled this roast
I've kept this hooker's half-deck damned genteel.
Si must ask pardon, or be made to squeal.
Down on your knees, dog; them we love we chasten.
Jao, pasea, my son—in English, Hasten.'

Si begged for pardon, meekly kneeling down
Before the reefer's mess assembled grim.
The lamp above them smoked the glass all brown;
Beyond the door the dripping sails were dim.
The Dauber passed the door; none spoke to him.
He sought his berth and slept, or, waking, heard
Rain on the deck-house—rain, no other word.

IV

OUT of the air a time of quiet came.
Calm fell upon the heaven like a drowth;
The brass sky watched the brassy water flame,
Drowsed as a snail the clipper loitered south
Slowly, with no white bone across her mouth,
No rushing glory, like a queen made bold,
The Dauber strove to draw her as she rolled.

There the four leaning spires of canvas rose,
Royals and skysails lifting, gently lifting,
White like the brightness that a great fish blows
When billows are at peace and ships are drifting;
With mighty jerks that set the shadows shifting,
The courses tugged their tethers: a blue haze
Drifted like ghosts of flocks come down to graze.

There the great skyline made her perfect round,
Notched now and then by the sea's deeper blue;
A smoke-smutch marked a steamer homeward bound.
The haze wrought all things to intenser hue.
In tingling impotence the Dauber drew
As all men draw, keen to the shaken soul
To give a hint that might suggest the whole.

A naked seaman washing a red shirt
Sat at a tub whistling between his teeth;
Complaining blocks quavered like something hurt,
A sailor cut an old boot for a sheath,
The ship bowed to her shadow-ship beneath,
And little slaps of spray came at the roll
On to the deck-planks from the scupper-hole.

He watched it, painting patiently, as paints
With eyes that pierce behind the blue sky's veil,
The Benedictine in a Book of Saints
Watching the passing of the Holy Grail;
The green dish dripping blood, the trump, the hail,
The spears that pass, the memory, and the passion,
The beauty moving under this world's fashion.

But as he painted, slowly, man by man,
The seamen gathered near; the Bosun stood
Behind him, jeering; then the Sails began
Sniggering with comment that it was not good.
Chips flicked his sketch with little scraps of wood,
Saying, 'That hit the top-knot,' every time.
Cook mocked, 'My lovely drawings; it's a crime.'

Slowly the men came nearer, till a crowd
Stood at his elbow, muttering as he drew;
The Bosun, turning to them, spoke aloud,
'This is the ship that never got there. You
Look at her here, what Dauber's trying to do.
Look at her! lummy, like a Christmas-tree.
That thing's a ship; he calls this painting. See?'

Seeing the crowd, the Mate came forward; then
'Sir,' said the Bosun, 'come and see the sight!
Here's Dauber makes a circus for the men.
He calls this thing a ship—this hell's delight!'
'Man,' said the Mate, 'you'll never get her right
Daubing like that. Look here!' He took a brush.
'Now, Dauber, watch; I'll put you to the blush.

'Look here. Look there. Now watch this ship of mine.'
He drew her swiftly from a memory stored.
'God, sir,' the Bosun said, 'you do her fine!'
'Ay,' said the Mate, 'I do so, by the Lord!
I'll paint a ship with any man aboard.'
They hung about his sketch like beasts at bait.
'There now, I taught him painting,' said the Mate.

When he had gone, the gathered men dispersed;
Yet two or three still lingered to dispute
What errors made the Dauber's work the worst.
They probed his want of knowledge to the root.
'Bei Gott!' they swore, 'der Dauber cannot do 't;
He haf no knolich how to put der pense.
Der Mate's is good. Der Dauber haf no sense.'

'You hear?' the Bosun cried, 'you cannot do it!'
'A gospel truth,' the Cook said, 'true as hell!
And wisdom, Dauber, if you only knew it;
A five year boy would do a ship as well.'
'If that's the kind of thing you hope to sell,
God help you,' echoed Chips. 'I tell you true
The job's beyond you, Dauber; drop it, do.

'Drop it, in God's name drop it, and have done!
You see you cannot do it. Here's the Mate
Paints you to frazzles before everyone;
Paints you a dandy clipper while you wait.
While you, Lord love us, daub. I tell you straight,
We've had enough of daubing; drop it; quit.
You cannot paint, so make an end of it.'

'That's sense,' said all; 'you cannot, why pretend?'
The Dauber rose and put his easel by.
'You've said enough,' he said, 'now let it end.
Who cares how bad my painting may be? I
Mean to go on, and, if I fail, to try.
However much I miss of my intent,
If I have done my best I'll be content.

'You cannot understand that. Let it be.
You cannot understand, nor know, nor share.
This is a matter touching only me;
My sketch may be a daub, for aught I care.
You may be right. But even if you were,
Your mocking should not stop this work of mine;
Rot though it be, its prompting is divine.

'You cannot understand that—you, and you,
And you, you Bosun. You can stand and jeer,
That is the task your spirit fits you to,
That you can understand and hold most dear.
Grin, then, like collars, ear to donkey ear,
But let me daub. Try, you, to understand
Which task will bear the light best on God's hand.'

V

THE wester came as steady as the Trades;
Brightly it blew, and still the ship did shoulder
The brilliance of the water's white cockades
Into the milky green of smoky smoulder.
The sky grew bluer and the air grew colder.
Southward she thundered while the westers held,
Proud, with taut bridles, pawing, but compelled.

And still the Dauber strove, though all men mocked,
To draw the splendour of the passing thing,
And deep inside his heart a something locked.
Long pricking in him, now began to sting—
A fear of the disasters storm might bring;
His rank as painter would be ended then—
He would keep watch and watch like other men.

And go aloft with them to man the yard
When the great ship was rolling scuppers under,
Burying her snout all round the compass card,
While the green water struck at her and stunned her;
When the lee-rigging slacked, when one long thunder
Boomed from the black to windward, when the sail
Booted and spurred the devil in the gale.

For him to ride on men: that was the time
The Dauber dreaded; then the test would come,
When seas, half-frozen, slushed the decks with slime,
And all the air was blind with flying scum;
When the drenched sails were furled, when the fierce hum
In weather riggings died into the roar
Of God's eternal never tamed by shore.

Once in the passage he had worked aloft,
Shifting her suits one summer afternoon,
In the bright Trade wind, when the wind was soft,
Shaking the points, making the tackle croon.
But that was child's play to the future: soon
He would be ordered up when sails and spars
Were flying and going mad among the stars.

He had been scared that first time, daunted, thrilled,
Not by the height so much as by the size,
And then the danger to the man unskilled
In standing on a rope that runs through eyes.
'But in a storm,' he thought, 'the yards will rise
And roll together down, and snap their gear!"
The sweat came cold upon his palms for fear.

Sometimes in Gloucester he had felt a pang
Swinging below the house-eaves on a stage.
But stages carry rails; here he would hang
Upon a jerking rope in a storm's rage,
Ducked that the sheltering oilskin might assuage
The beating of the storm, clutching the jack,
Beating the sail, and being beaten back.

Drenched, frozen, gasping, blinded, beaten dumb,
High in the night, reeling great blinding arcs
As the ship rolled, his chappy fingers numb,
The deck below a narrow blur of marks,
The sea a welter of whiteness shot with sparks,
Now snapping up in bursts, now dying away,
Salting the horizontal snow with spray.

A hundred and fifty feet above the deck,
And there, while the ship rolls, boldly to sit
Upon a foot-rope moving, jerk and check,
While half a dozen seamen work on it;
Held by one hand, straining, by strength and wit
To toss a gasket's coil around the yard,
How could he compass that when blowing hard?

And if he failed in any least degree,
Or faltered for an instant, or showed slack,
He might go drown himself within the sea,
And add a bubble to the clipper's track.
He had signed his name, there was no turning back,
No pardon for default—this must be done.
One iron rule at sea binds everyone.

Till now he had been treated with contempt
As neither man nor thing, a creature borne
On the ship's articles, but left exempt
From all the seamen's life except their scorn.
But he would rank as seaman off the Horn,
Work as a seaman, and be kept or cast
By standards set for men before the mast.

Even now they shifted suits of sails; they bent
The storm-suit ready for the expected time;
The mighty wester that the Plate had lent
Had brought them far into the wintry clime.
At dawn, out of the shadow, there was rime,
The dim Magellan Clouds were frosty clear,
The wind had edge, the testing-time was near.

And then he wondered if the tales were lies
Told by old hands to terrify the new,
For, since the ship left England, only twice
Had there been need to start a sheet or clew,
Then only royals, for an hour or two,
And no seas broke aboard, nor was it cold.
What were these gales of which the stories told?

The thought went by. He had heard the Bosun tell
Too often, and too fiercely, not to know
That being off the Horn in June is hell:
Hell of continual toil in ice and snow,
Frost-bitten hell in which the westers blow
Shrieking for days on end, in which the seas
Gulf the starved seamen till their marrows freeze.

Such was the weather he might look to find,
Such was the work expected: there remained
Firmly to set his teeth, resolve his mind,
And be the first, however much it pained,
And bring his honour round the Horn unstained,
And win his mates' respect; and thence, untainted,
Be ranked as man however much he painted.

He drew deep breath; a gantline swayed aloft
A lower topsail, hard with rope and leather
Such as men's frozen fingers fight with oft
Below the Ramirez in Cape Horn weather.
The arms upon the yard hove all together,
Lighting the head along; a thought occurred
Within the painter's brain like a bright bird:

That this, and so much like it, of man's toil,
Compassed by naked manhood in strange places,
Was all heroic, but outside the coil
Within which modern art gleams or grimaces;
That if he drew that line of sailors' faces
Sweating the sail, their passionate play and change,
It would be new, and wonderful, and strange.

That that was what his work meant; it would be
A training in new vision—a revealing
Of passionate men in battle with the sea,
High on an unseen stage, shaking and reeling;
And men through him would understand their feeling,
Their might, their misery, their tragic power,
And all by suffering pain a little hour;

High on the yard with them, feeling their pain,
Battling with them; and it had not been done.
He was a door to new worlds in the brain,
A window opening letting in the sun,
A voice saying, 'Thus is bread fetched and ports won
And life lived out at sea where men exist
Solely by man's strong brain and sturdy wrist.'

So he decided, as he cleaned his brasses,
Hearing without, aloft, the curse, the shout
Where the taut gantline passes and repasses,
Heaving new topsails to be lighted out.
It was most proud, however self might doubt,
To share man's tragic toil and paint it true.
He took the offered Fate: this he would do.

That night the snow fell between six and seven.
A little feathery fall so light, so dry—
An aimless dust out of a confused heaven,
Upon an air no steadier than a sigh;
The powder dusted down and wandered by
So purposeless, so many, and so cold,
Then died, and the wind ceased and the ship rolled.

Rolled till she clanged—rolled till the brain was tired,
Marking the acme of the heaves, the pause
While the sea-beauty rested and respired,
Drinking great draughts of roller at her hawse.
Flutters of snow came aimless upon flaws.
'Lock up your paints,' the Mate said, speaking light:
'This is the Horn; you'll join my watch to-night!'

VI

ALL through the windless night the clipper rolled
In a great swell with oily gradual heaves
Which rolled her down until her time-bells tolled,
Clang, and the weltering water moaned like beeves.
The thundering rattle of slatting shook the sheaves,
Startles of water made the swing ports gush,
The sea was moaning and sighing and saying 'Hush!'

It was all black and starless. Peering down
Into the water, trying to pierce the gloom,
One saw a dim, smooth, oily glitter of brown
Heaving and dying away and leaving room
For yet another. Like the march of doom
Came those great powers of marching silences;
Then fog came down, dead-cold, and hid the seas.

They set the Dauber to the foghorn. There
He stood upon the poop, making to sound
Out of the pump the sailors' nasal blare,
Listening lest ice should make the note resound.
She bayed there like a solitary hound
Lost in a covert; all the watch she bayed,
The fog, come closelier down, no answer made.

Denser it grew, until the ship was lost.
The elemental hid her; she was merged
In mufflings of dark death, like a man's ghost,
New to the change of death, yet thither urged.
Then from the hidden waters something surged—
Mournful, despairing, great, greater than speech,
A noise like one slow wave on a still beach.

Mournful, and then again mournful, and still
Out of the night that mighty voice arose;
The Dauber at his foghorn felt the thrill.
Who rode that desolate sea? What forms were those?
Mournful, from things defeated, in the throes
Of memory of some conquered hunting-ground,
Out of the night of death arose the sound.

'Whales!' said the mate. They stayed there all night long
Answering the horn. Out of the night they spoke,
Defeated creatures who had suffered wrong,
But were still noble underneath the stroke.
They filled the darkness when the Dauber woke;
The men came peering to the rail to hear,
And the sea sighed, and the fog rose up sheer.

A wall of nothing at the world's last edge,
Where no life came except defeated life.
The Dauber felt shut in within a hedge,
Behind which form was hidden and thought was rife,
And that a blinding flash, a thrust, a knife
Would sweep the hedge away and make all plain,
Brilliant beyond all words, blinding the brain.

D.—4

So the night past, but then no morning broke—
Only a something showed that night was dead.
A sea-bird, cackling like a devil, spoke,
And the fog drew away and hung like lead.
Like mighty cliffs it shaped, sullen and red;
Like glowering gods at watch it did appear,
And sometimes drew away, and then drew near.

Like islands, and like chasms, and like hell,
But always mighty and red, gloomy and ruddy,
Shutting the visible sea in like a well;
Slow heaving in vast ripples, blank and muddy,
Where the sun should have risen it streaked bloody.
The day was still-born: all the sea-fowl scattering
Splashed the still water, mewing, hovering, clattering.

Then Polar snow came down little and light,
Till all the sky was hidden by the small,
Most multudinous drift of dirty white
Tumbling and wavering down and covering all—
Covering the sky, the sea, the clipper tall,
Furring the ropes with white, casing the mast,
Coming on no known air, but blowing past.

And all the air seemed full of gradual moan,
As though in those cloud-chasms the horns were blowing
The mort for gods cast out and overthrown,
Or for the eyeless sun plucked out and going.
Slow the low gradual moan came in the snowing;
The Dauber felt the prelude had begun.
The snowstorm fluttered by; he saw the sun

Show and pass by, gleam from one towering prison
Into another, vaster and more grim,
Which in dull crags of darkness had arisen
To muffle-to a final door on him.
The gods upon the dull crags lowered dim,
The pigeons chattered, quarrelling in the track.
In the south-west the dimness dulled to black.

Then came the cry of 'Call all hands on deck!'
The Dauber knew its meaning; it was come:
Cape Horn, that tramples beauty into wreck,
And crumples steel and smites the strong man dumb.
Down clattered flying kites and staysails: some
Sang out in quick, high calls; the fairleads skirled,
And from the south-west came the end of the world.

'Caught in her ball-dress,' said the Bosun, hauling;
'Lee-ay, lee-ay!' quick, high, came the men's call;
It was all wallop of sails and startled calling.
'Let fly!' 'Let go!' 'Clew up!' and 'Let go all!'
'Now up and make them fast!' 'Here, give us a haul!'
'Now up and stow them! Quick! By God! we're done!'
The blackness crunched all memory of the sun.

'Up!' said the Mate. 'Mizen topgallants. Hurry!'
The Dauber ran, the others ran, the sails
Slatted and shook; out of the black a flurry
Whirled in fine lines, tattering the edge to trails.
Painting and art and England were old tales
Told in some other life to that pale man,
Who struggled with white fear and gulped and ran.

He struck a ringbolt in his haste and fell—
Rose, sick with pain, half-lamed in his left knee;
He reached the shrouds where clambering men pell-mell
Hustled each other up and cursed him; he
Hurried aloft with them: then from the sea
Came a cold, sudden breath that made the hair
Stiff on the neck, as though Death whispered there.

A man below him punched him in the side.
'Get up, you Dauber, or let me get past.'
He saw the belly of the skysail skied,
Gulped, and clutched tight, and tried to go more fast.
Sometimes he missed his ratline and was grassed,
Scraped his shin raw against the rigid line.
The clamberers reached the futtock-shrouds' incline.

Cursing they came; one kicking out behind,
Kicked Dauber in the mouth, and one below
Punched at his calves; the futtock-shrouds inclined,
It was a perilous path for one to go.
'Up, Dauber, up!' A curse followed a blow.
He reached the top and gasped, then on, then on.
And one voice yelled 'Let go!' and one 'All gone!'

Fierce clamberers, some in oilskins, some in rags,
Hustling and hurrying up, up the steep stairs.
Before the windless sails were blown to flags,
And whirled like dirty birds athwart great airs,
Ten men in all, to get this mast of theirs
Snugged to the gale in time. 'Up! Damn you, run!
The mizen topmast head was safely won.

'Lay out!' the Bosun yelled. The Dauber laid
Out on the yard, gripping the yard, and feeling
Sick at the mighty space of air displayed
Below his feet, where mewing birds were wheeling.
A giddy fear was on him; he was reeling.
He bit his lip half through, clutching the jack.
A cold sweat glued the shirt upon his back.

The yard was shaking, for a brace was loose.
He felt that he would fall; he clutched, he bent,
Clammy with natural terror to the shoes
While idiotic promptings came and went.
Snow fluttered on a wind-flaw and was spent;
He saw the water darken. Someone yelled,
'Frap it; don't stay to furl! Hold on!' He held.

Darkness came down—half darkness—in a whirl;
The sky went out, the waters disappeared.
He felt a shocking pressure of blowing hurl
The ship upon her side. The darkness speared
At her with wind; she staggered, she careered,
Then down she lay. The Dauber felt her go;
He saw his yard tilt downwards. Then the snow

Whirled all about—dense, multitudinous, cold—
Mixed with the wind's one devilish thrust and shriek,
Which whiffled out men's tears, deafened, took hold,
Flattening the flying drift against the cheek.
The yards buckled and bent, man could not speak.
The ship lay on her broadside; the wind's sound
Had devilish malice at having got her downed.

*   *   *

How long the gale had blown he could not tell,
Only the world had changed, his life had died.
A moment now was everlasting hell.
Nature an onslaught from the weather side,
A withering rush of death, a frost that cried,
Shrieked, till he withered at the heart; a hail
Plastered his oilskins with an icy mail.

'Cut!' yelled his mate. He looked—the sail was shred
Blown into rags in the first furious squall;
The tatters into tongues and stringers spread
A block upon the yard thumped like a mall.
The ship lay—the sea smote her, the wind's bawl
Came, 'loo, loo, loo!' The devil cried his hounds
On to the poor spent stag strayed in his bounds.

'Cut! Ease her!' yelled his mate; the Dauber heard.
His mate wormed up the tilted yard and slashed,
A rag of canvas skimmed like a darting bird.
The snow whirled, the ship bowed to it, the gear lashed,
The sea-tops were cut off and flung down smashed;
Tatters of shouts were flung, the rags of yells—
And clang, clang, clang, below beat the two bells.

'O God!' the Dauber moaned. A roaring rang,
Blasting the royals like a cannonade;
The backstays parted with a cracking clang,
The upper spars were snapped like twigs decayed—
Snapped at their heels, their jagged splinters splayed,
Like white and ghastly hair erect with fear.
The Mate yelled, 'Gone, by God, and pitched them clear!'

'Up!' yelled the Bosun; 'up and clear the wreck!'
The Dauber followed where he led: below
He caught one giddy glimpsing of the deck
Filled with white water, as though heaped with snow.
He saw the streamers of the rigging blow
Straight out like pennons from the splintered mast,
Then, all sense dimmed, all was an icy blast.

Roaring from nether hell and filled with ice,
Roaring and crashing on the jerking stage,
An utter bridle given to utter vice,
Limitless power mad with endless rage
Withering the soul; a minute seemed an age.
He clutched and hacked at ropes, at rags of sail,
Thinking that comfort was a fairy-tale

Told long ago—long, long ago—long since
Heard of in other lives—imagined, dreamed—
There where the basest beggar was a prince
To him in torment where the tempest screamed,
Comfort and warmth and ease no longer seemed
Things that a man could know: soul, body, brain,
Knew nothing but the wind, the cold, the pain.

'Leave that!' the Bosun shouted: 'Crojick save!'
The splitting crojick, not yet gone to rags,
Thundered below, beating till something gave,
Bellying between its buntlines into bags.
Some birds were blown past, shrieking: dark, like shags,
Their backs seemed, looking down. 'Leu, leu!' they cried.
The ship lay, the seas thumped her; she had died.

They reached the crojick yard, which buckled, buckled
Like a thin whalebone to the topsail's strain.
They laid upon the yard and heaved and knuckled,
Pounding the sail, which jangled and leapt again.
It was quite hard with ice, its rope like chain,
Its strength like seven devils; it shook the mast.
They cursed and toiled and froze: a long time passed

Two hours passed, then a dim lightening came.
Those frozen ones upon the yard could see
The mainsail and the foresail still the same,
Still battling with the hands and blowing free,
Rags tattered where the staysails used to be.
The lower topsails stood; the ship's lee deck
Seethed with four feet of water filled with wreck.

An hour more went by; the Dauber lost
All sense of hands and feet, all sense of all
But of a wind that cut him to the ghost,
And of a frozen fold he had to haul,
Of heavens that fell and never ceased to fall,
And ran in smoky snatches along the sea,
Leaping from crest to wave-crest, yelling. He

Lost sense of time; no bells went, but he felt
Ages go over him. At last, at last
They frapped the cringled crojick's icy pelt;
In frozen bulge and bunt they made it fast.
Then, scarcely live, they laid in to the mast.
The Captain's speaking-trumpet gave a blare,
'Make fast the topsail, Mister, while you're there.'

Some seamen cursed, but up they had to go—
Up to the topsail yard to spend an hour
Stowing a topsail in a blinding snow,
Which made the strongest man among them cower.
More men came up, the fresh hands gave them power,
They stowed the sail; then with a rattle of chain
One half the crojick burst its bonds again.

★   ★   ★

They stowed the sail, frapping it round with rope,
Leaving no surface for the wind, no fold,
Then down the weather-shrouds, half dead, they grope;
That struggle with the sail had made them old.
They wondered if the crojick furl would hold.
'Lucky,' said one, 'it didn't spring the spar.'
'Lucky,' the Bosun said, 'lucky! We are!

She came within two shakes of turning top
Or stripping all her shroud-screws, that first quiff.
Now fish those wash-deck buckets out of the slop.
Here's Dauber says he doesn't like Cape Stiff.
This isn't wind, man, this is only a whiff.
Hold on, all hands, hold on!' a sea, half seen,
Paused, mounted, burst, and filled the main-deck green.

The Dauber felt a mountain of water fall.
It covered him deep, deep, he felt it fill,
Over his head, the deck, the fife-rails, all,
Quieting the ship, she trembled and lay still.
Then with a rush and shatter and clanging shrill
Over she went; he saw the water cream
Over the bitts; he saw the half-deck stream.

Then in the rush he swirled, over she went;
Her lee-rail dipped, he struck, and something gave;
His legs went through a port as the roll spent;
She paused, then rolled, and back the water drave.
He drifted with it as a part of the wave,
Drowning, half-stunned, exhausted, partly frozen,
He struck the booby hatchway; then the Bosun

Leaped, seeing his chance, before the next sea burst,
And caught him as he drifted, seized him, held,
Up-ended him against the bitts, and cursed.
'This ain't the George's Swimming Baths,' he yelled;
'Keep on your feet!' Another grey-back felled
The two together, and the Bose, half-blind,
Spat: 'One's a joke,' he cursed, 'but two's unkind.'

'Now, damn it, Dauber!' said the Mate. 'Look out,
Or you'll be over the side!' The water freed;
Each clanging freeing-port became a spout.
The men cleared up the decks as there was need.
The Dauber's head was cut, he felt it bleed
Into his oilskins as he clutched and coiled.
Water and sky were devils' brews which boiled,

Boiled, shrieked, and glowered; but the ship was saved,
Snugged safely down, though fourteen sails were split.
Out of the dark a fiercer fury raved.
The grey-backs died and mounted, each crest lit
With a white toppling gleam that hissed from it
And slid, or leaped, or ran with whirls of cloud,
Mad with inhuman life that shrieked aloud.

The watch was called; Dauber might go below.
'Splice the main brace!' the Mate called. All laid aft
To get a gulp of momentary glow
As some reward for having saved the craft.
The steward ladled mugs, from which each quaffed
Whisky, with water, sugar, and lime-juice, hot,
A quarter of a pint each made the tot.

Beside the lamp-room door the steward stood
Ladling it out, and each man came in turn,
Tipped his sou'-wester, drank it, grunted 'Good!'
And shambled forward, letting it slowly burn.
When all were gone the Dauber lagged astern,
Torn by his frozen body's lust for heat,
The liquor's pleasant smell, so warm, so sweet,

And by a promise long since made at home
Never to taste strong liquor. Now he knew
The worth of liquor; now he wanted some.
His frozen body urged him to the brew;
Yet it seemed wrong, an evil thing to do
To break that promise. 'Dauber,' said the Mate,
'Drink, and turn in, man; why the hell d'ye wait?'

'Please, sir, I'm temperance.' 'Temperance are you, hey?
That's all the more for me! So you're for slops?
I thought you'd had enough slops for to-day.
Go to your bunk and ease her when she drops.
And—damme, steward! you brew with too much hops!
Stir up the sugar, man!—and tell your girl
How kind the Mate was teaching you to furl.'

Then the Mate drank the remnants, six men's share,
And ramped into his cabin, where he stripped
And danced unclad, and was uproarious there.
In waltzes with the cabin cat he tripped,
Singing in tenor clear that he was pipped—
That 'he who strove the tempest to disarm,
Must never first embrail the lee yard-arm,'

And that his name was Ginger. Dauber crept
Back to the round-house, gripping by the rail.
The wind howled by; the passionate water leapt;
The night was all one roaring with the gale.
Then at the door he stopped, uttering a wail;
His hands were perished numb and blue as veins.
He could not turn the knob for both the Spains.

A hand came shuffling aft, dodging the seas,
Singing 'her nut-brown hair' between his teeth;
Taking the ocean's tumult at his ease
Even when the wash about his thighs did seethe.
His soul was happy in its happy sheath;
'What, Dauber, won't it open? Fingers cold?
You'll talk of this time, Dauber, when you're old.'

He flung the door half open, and a sea
Washed them both in, over the splashboard, down
'You silly, salt miscarriage!' sputtered he.
'Dauber, pull out the plug before we drown!
That's spoiled my laces and my velvet gown.
Where is the plug?' Groping in pitch dark water,
He sang between his teeth 'The Farmer's Daughter'.

It was pitch dark within there; at each roll
The chests slid to the slant; the water rushed,
Making full many a clanging tin pan bowl
Into the black below-bunks as it gushed.
The dog-tired men slept through it; they were hushed.
The water drained, and then with matches damp
The man struck heads off till he lit the lamp.

'Thank you,' the Dauber said; the seaman grinned.
'This is your first foul weather?' 'Yes.' 'I thought
Up on the yard you hadn't seen much wind.
Them's rotten sea-boots, Dauber, that you brought.
Now I must cut on deck before I'm caught.'
He went; the lamp-flame smoked; he slammed the door;
A film of water loitered across the floor.

The Dauber watched it come and watched it go;
He had had revelation of the lies
Cloaking the truth men never choose to know;
He could bear witness now and cleanse their eyes
He had beheld in suffering; he was wise;
This was the sea, this searcher of the soul—
This never-dying shriek fresh from the Pole.

He shook with cold; his hands could not undo
His oilskin buttons, so he shook and sat,
Watching his dirty fingers, dirty blue,
Hearing without the hammering tackle slat,
Within, the drops from dripping clothes went pat,
Running in little patters, gentle, sweet,
And 'Ai, ai!' went the wind, and the seas beat.

His bunk was sopping wet; he clambered in.
None of his clothes were dry; his fear recurred.
Cramps bunched the muscles underneath his skin.
The great ship rolled until the lamp was blurred.
He took his Bible and tried to read a word;
Trembled at going aloft again, and then
Resolved to fight it out and show it to men.

Faces recurred, fierce memories of the yard,
The frozen sail, the savage eyes, the jests,
The oaths of one great seaman syphilis-scarred,
The tug of leeches jammed beneath their chests,
The buntlines bellying bunts out into breasts.
The deck so desolate-grey, the sky so wild,
He fell asleep, and slept like a young child.

But not for long; the cold awoke him soon,
The hot-ache and the skin-cracks and the cramp,
The seas thundering without, the gale's wild tune,
The sopping misery of the blankets damp.
A speaking-trumpet roared; a sea-boot's stamp
Clogged at the door. A man entered to shout:
'All hands on deck! Arouse here! Tumble out!'

The caller raised the lamp; his oilskins clicked
As the thin ice upon them cracked and fell.
'Rouse out!' he said. 'This lamp is frozen wicked.
Rouse out!' His accent deepened to a yell.
'We're among ice; it's blowing up like hell.
We're going to hand both topsails. Time, I guess,
We're sheeted up. Rouse out! Don't stay to dress!'

'Is it cold on deck?' said Dauber. 'Is it cold?
We're sheeted up, I tell you, inches thick!
The fo'c's'le's like a wedding-cake, I'm told.
Now tumble out, my sons; on deck here, quick!
Rouse out, away, and come and climb the stick.
I'm going to call the half-deck. Bosun! Hey!
Both topsails coming in. Heave out! Away!'

He went; the Dauber tumbled from his bunk,
Clutching the side. He heard the wind go past,
Making the great ship wallow as if drunk.
There was a shocking tumult up the mast.
'This is the end,' he muttered, 'come at last!
I've got to go aloft, facing this cold.
I can't. I can't. I'll never keep my hold.

'I cannot face the topsail yard again.
I never guessed what misery it would be.'
The cramps and hot-ache made him sick with pain.
The ship stopped suddenly from a devilish sea,
Then, with a triumph of wash, a rush of glee,
The door burst in, and in the water rolled,
Filling the lower bunks, black, creaming, cold.

The lamp sucked out. 'Wash!' went the water back,
Then in again, flooding; the Bosun swore.
'You useless thing! You Dauber! You lee slack!
Get out, you heekapoota! Shut the door!
You coo-ilyaira, what are you waiting for?
Out of my way, you thing—you useless thing!'
He slammed the door indignant, clanging the ring.

And then he lit the lamp, drowned to the waist;
'Here's a fine house! Get at the scupper-holes'—
He bent against it as the water raced—
'And pull them out to leeward when she rolls.
They say some kinds of landsmen don't have souls.
I well believe. A Port Mahon baboon
Would make more soul than you got with a spoon.'

Down in the icy water Dauber groped
To find the plug; the racing water sluiced
Over his head and shoulders as she sloped.
Without, judged by the sound, all hell was loosed,
He felt cold Death about him tightly noosed.
That Death was better than the misery there
Iced on the quaking foothold high in air.

And then the thought came: 'I'm a failure. All
My life has been a failure. They were right.
It will not matter if I go and fall;
I should be free then from this hell's delight.
I'll never paint. Best let it end to-night.
I'll slip over the side. I've tried and failed.'
So in the ice-cold in the night he quailed.

Death would be better, death, than this long hell
Of mockery and surrender and dismay—
This long defeat of doing nothing well,
Playing the part too high for him to play.
'O Death! who hides the sorry thing away,
Take me; I've failed. I cannot play these cards.'
There came a thundering from the topsail yards.

And then he bit his lips, clenching his mind,
And staggered out to muster, beating back
The coward frozen self of him that whined.
Come what cards might he meant to play the pack.
'Ai!' screamed the wind; the topsail sheets went clack;
Ice filled the air with spikes; the grey-backs burst.
'Here's Dauber,' said the Mate, 'on deck the first.

'Why, holy sailor, Dauber, you're a man!
I took you for a soldier. Up now, come!'
Up on the yards already they began
That battle with a gale which strikes men dumb
The leaping topsail thundered like a drum.
The frozen snow beat in the face like shots.
The wind spun whipping wave-crests into clots.

So up upon the topsail yard again,
In the great tempest's fiercest hour, began
Probation to the Dauber's soul, of pain
Which crowds a century's torment in a span.
For the next month the ocean taught this man,
And he, in that month's torment, while she wested,
Was never warm nor dry, nor full nor rested.

But still it blew, or, if it lulled, it rose
Within the hour and blew again; and still
The water as it burst aboard her froze.
The wind blew off an ice-field, raw and chill,
Daunting man's body, tampering with his will;
But after thirty days a ghostly sun
Gave sickly promise that the storms were done.

D.—5

VII

A GREAT grey sea was running up the sky,
Desolate birds flew past; their mewings came
As that lone water's spiritual cry,
Its forlorn voice, its essence, its soul's name.
The ship limped in the water as if lame.
Then in the forenoon watch to a great shout
More sail was made, the reefs were shaken out.

A slant came from the south; the singers stood
Clapped to the halliards, hauling to a tune,
Old as the sea, a fillip to the blood.
The upper topsail rose like a balloon.
'So long, Cape Stiff. In Valparaiso soon,'
Said one to other, as the ship lay over,
Making her course again—again a rover.

Slowly the sea went down as the wind fell.
Clear rang the songs, 'Hurrah! Cape Horn is bet!'
The combless seas were lumping into swell;
The leaking fo'c's'les were no longer wet.
More sail was made; the watch on deck was set
To cleaning up the ruin broken bare
Below, aloft, about her, everywhere.

The Dauber, scrubbing out the round-house, found
Old pantiles pulped among the mouldy gear,
Washed underneath the bunks and long since drowned
During the agony of the Cape Horn year.
He sang in scrubbing, for he had done with fear—
Fronted the worst and looked it in the face;
He had got manhood at the testing-place.

Singing he scrubbed, passing his watch below,
Making the round-house fair; the Bosun watched,
Bringing his knitting slowly to the toe.
Sails stretched a mizen skysail which he patched;
They thought the Dauber was a bad egg hatched.
'Daubs,' said the Bosun cheerly, 'can you knit?
I've made a Barney's Bull of this last bit.'

Then, while the Dauber counted, Bosun took
Some marline from his pocket. 'Here,' he said,
'You want to know square sennit? So fash. Look!
Eight foxes take, and stop the ends with thread.
I've known an engineer would give his head
To know square sennit.' As the Bose began,
The Dauber felt promoted into man.

It was his warrant that he had not failed—
That the most hard part in his difficult climb
Had not been past attainment; it was scaled:
Safe footing showed above the slippery slime.
He had emerged out of the iron time,
And knew that he could compass his life's scheme
He had the power sufficient to his dream.

Then dinner came, and now the sky was blue.
The ship was standing north, the Horn was rounded;
She made a thundering as she weltered through.
The mighty grey-backs glittered as she bounded.
More sail was piled upon her; she was hounded
North, while the wind came; like a stag she ran
Over grey hills and hollows of seas wan.

She had a white bone in her mouth: she sped;
Those in the round-house watched her as they ate
Their meal of pork-fat fried with broken bread.
'Good old!' they cried. 'She's off; she's gathering gait!'
Her track was whitening like a Lammas spate.
'Good old!' they cried. 'Oh, give her cloth! Hurray!
For three weeks more to Valparaiso Bay!'

'She smells old Vallipo,' the Bosun cried.
'We'll be inside the tier in three weeks more,
Lying at double-moorings where they ride
Off of the market, half a mile from shore,
And bumboat pan, my sons, and figs galore,
And girls in black mantillas fit to make a
Poor seaman frantic when they dance the cueca.'

Eight bells were made, the watch was changed, and now
The Mate spoke to the Dauber: 'This is better.
We'll soon be getting mudhooks over the bow.
She'll make her passage still if this'll let her.
Oh, run, you drogher! dip your fo'c's'le wetter.
Well, Dauber, this is better than Cape Horn.
Them topsails made you wish you'd not been born.'

'Yes, sir,' the Dauber said. 'Now,' said the Mate,
'We've got to smart her up. Them Cape Horn seas
Have made her paint-work like a rusty grate.
Oh, didn't them topsails make your fish-hooks freeze?
A topsail don't pay heed to "Won't you, please?"
Well, you have seen Cape Horn, my son; you've learned.
You've dipped your hand and had your fingers burned.

'And now you'll stow that folly, trying to paint.
You've had your lesson; you're a sailor now.
You come on board a female ripe to faint.
All sorts of slush you'd learned, the Lord knows how.
Cape Horn has sent you wisdom over the bow
If you've got sense to take it. You're a sailor.
My God! before, you were a woman's tailor.

'So throw your paints to blazes and have done.
Words can't describe the silly things you did
Sitting before your easel in the sun,
With all your colours on the paint-box lid.
I blushed for you . . . and then the daubs you hid.
My God! you'll have more sense now, eh? You've quit?'
'No, sir.' 'You've not?' 'No, sir.' 'God give you wit.

'I thought you'd come to wisdom.' Thus they talked,
While the great clipper took her bit and rushed
Like a skin-glistening stallion not yet baulked,
Till fire-bright water at her swing-ports gushed;
Poising and bowing down her fore-foot crushed
Bubble on glittering bubble; on she went.
The Dauber watched her, wondering what it meant.

To come, after long months, at rosy dawn,
Into the placid blue of some great bay.
Treading the quiet water like a fawn
Ere yet the morning haze was blown away.
A rose-flushed figure putting by the grey,
And anchoring there before the city smoke
Rose, or the church-bells rang, or men awoke.

And then, in the first light, to see grow clear
That long-expected haven filled with strangers—
Alive with men and women; see and hear
Its clattering market and its money-changers;
And hear the surf beat, and be free from dangers,
And watch the crinkled ocean blue with calm
Drowsing beneath the Trade, beneath the palm.

Hungry for that he worked; the hour went by,
And still the wind grew, still the clipper strode,
And now a darkness hid the western sky,
And sprays came flicking off at the wind's goad.
She stumbled now, feeling her sail a load.
The Mate gazed hard to windward, eyed his sail,
And said the Horn was going to flick her tail.

Boldly he kept it on her till she staggered,
But still the wind increased; it grew, it grew,
Darkening the sky, making the water haggard:
Full of small snow the mighty wester blew.
'More fun for little fish-hooks,' sighed the crew.
They eyed the taut topgallants stiff like steel;
A second hand was ordered to the wheel.

The Captain eyed her aft, sucking his lip,
Feeling the sail too much, but yet refraining
From putting hobbles on the leaping ship,
The glad sea-shattering stallion, halter-straining,
Wind-musical, uproarious, and complaining;
But, in a gust, he cocked his finger, so:
'You'd better take them off, before they go.'

All saw. They ran at once without the word
'Leeay! Leeay!' Loud rang the clew-line cries;
Sam in his bunk within the half-deck heard,
Stirred in his sleep, and rubbed his drowsy eyes.
'There go the lower to'gallants.' Against the skies
Rose the thin bellying strips of leaping sail.
The Dauber was the first man over the rail.

Three to a mast they ran; it was a race.
'God!' said the Mate; 'that Dauber, he can go.'
He watched the runners with an upturned face
Over the futtocks, struggling heel to toe,
Up to the topmast cross-trees into the blow
Where the three sails were leaping. 'Dauber wins!'
The yards were reached, and now the race begins.

Which three will furl their sail first and come down?
Out to the yard-arm for the leech goes one,
His hair blown flagwise from a hatless crown,
His hands at work like fever to be done.
Out of the gale a fiercer fury spun.
The three sails leaped together, yanking high,
Like talons darting up to clutch the sky.

The Dauber on the fore topgallant yard
Out at the weather yard-arm was the first
To lay his hand upon the buntline-barred
Topgallant yanking to the wester's burst;
He craned to catch the leech; his comrades cursed;
One at the buntlines, one with oaths observed,
'The eye of the outer jib-stay isn't served.'

'No,' said the Dauber. 'No,' the man replied.
They heaved, stowing the sail, not looking round,
Panting, but full of life and eager-eyed;
The gale roared at them with its iron sound.
'That's you,' the Dauber said. His gasket wound
Swift round the yard, binding the sail in bands;
There came a gust, the sail leaped from his hands,

So that he saw it high above him, grey,
And there his mate was falling; quick he clutched
An arm in oilskins swiftly snatched away.
A voice said 'Christ!' a quick shape stooped and touched,
Chain struck his hands, ropes shot, the sky was smutched
With vast black fires that ran, that fell, that furled,
And then he saw the mast, the small snow hurled.

The fore topgallant yard far, far aloft,
And blankness settling on him and great pain;
And snow beneath his fingers wet and soft
And topsail-sheet-blocks shaking at the chain.
He knew it was he who had fallen; then his brain
Swirled in a circle while he watched the sky.
Infinite multitudes of snow blew by.

'I thought it was Tom who fell,' his brain's voice said
'Down on the bloody deck!' the Captain screamed.
The multitudinous little snow-flakes sped,
His pain was real enough, but all else seemed.
Si with a bucket ran, the water gleamed
Tilting upon him; others came, the Mate . . .
They knelt with eager eyes like things that wait

For other things to come. He saw them there.
'It will go on,' he murmured, watching Si.
Colours and sounds seemed mixing in the air,
The pain was stunning him, and the wind went by.
'More water,' said the Mate. 'Here, Bosun, try.
Ask if he's got a message. Hell, he's gone!
Here, Dauber, Paints.' He said, 'It will go on.'

Not knowing his meaning rightly, but he spoke
With the intenseness of a fading soul
Whose share of Nature's fire turns to smoke,
Whose hand on Nature's wheel loses control.
The eager faces glowered red like coal.
They glowed, the great storm glowed, the sails, the mast.
'It will go on,' he cried aloud, and passed.

Those from the yard came down to tell the tale.
'He almost had me off,' said Tom. 'He slipped.
There came one hell of a jump-like from the sail. . . .
He clutched at me and almost had me pipped.
He caught my 'ris'band, but the oilskin ripped. . . .
It tore clean off. Look here. I was near gone.
I made a grab to catch him; so did John.

'I caught his arm. My God! I was near done.
He almost had me over; it was near.
He hit the ropes and grabbed at every one.'
'Well,' said the Mate, 'we cannot leave him here.
Run, Si, and get the half-deck table clear.
We'll lay him there. Catch hold there, you, and you.
He's dead, poor son; there's nothing more to do.'

Night fell, and all night long the Dauber lay
Covered upon the table; all night long
The pitiless storm exulted at her prey,
Huddling the waters with her icy thong.
But to the covered shape she did no wrong.
He lay beneath the sailcloth. Bell by bell
The night wore through; the stars rose, the stars fell.

Blowing most pitiless cold out of clear sky
The wind roared all night long; and all night through
The green seas on the deck went washing by,
Flooding the half-deck; bitter hard it blew.
But little of it all the Dauber knew—
The sopping bunks, the floating chests, the wet
The darkness, and the misery, and the sweat.

He was off duty. So it blew all night,
And when the watches changed the men would come
Dripping within the door to strike a light
And stare upon the Dauber lying dumb,
And say, 'He come a cruel thump, poor chum.'
Or, 'He'd a-been a fine big man'; or, 'He . . .
A smart young seaman he was getting to be.'

Or, 'Damn it all, it's what we've all to face! . . .
I knew another fellow one time . . .' then
Came a strange tale of death in a strange place
Out on the sea, in ships, with wandering men.
In many ways Death puts us into pen.
The reefers came down tired and looked and slept.
Below the skylight little dribbles crept

Along the painted woodwork, glistening, slow,
Following the roll and dripping, never fast,
But dripping on the quiet form below,
Like passing time talking to time long past.
And all night long 'Ai, ai!' went the wind's blast,
And creaming water swished below the pale,
Unheeding body stretched beneath the sail.

At dawn they sewed him up, and at eight bells
They bore him to the gangway, wading deep,
Through the green-clutching, white-toothed water-hells
That flung his carriers over in their sweep.
They laid an old red ensign on the heap,
And all hands stood bare-headed, stooping, swaying,
Washed by the sea while the old man was praying.

Out of a borrowed prayer-book. At a sign
They twitched the ensign back and tipped the grating.
A creamier bubbling broke the bubbling brine.
The muffled figure tilted to the weighting;
It dwindled slowly down, slowly gyrating.
Some craned to see; it dimmed, it disappeared;
The last green milky bubble blinked and cleared.

'Mister, shake out your reefs,' the Captain called.
'Out topsail reefs!' the Mate cried; then all hands.
Hurried, the great sails shook, and all hands hauled,
Singing that desolate song of lonely lands,
Of how a lover came in dripping bands,
Green with the wet and cold, to tell his lover
That Death was in the sea, and all was over.

Fair came the falling wind; a seaman said
The Dauber was a Jonah; once again
The clipper held her course, showing red lead,
Shattering the sea-tops into golden rain.
The waves bowed down before her like blown grain;
Onwards she thundered, on; her voyage was short,
Before the tier's bells rang her into port.

Cheerly they rang her in, those beating bells,
The new-come beauty stately from the sea,
Whitening the blue heave of the drowsy swells,
Treading the bubbles down. With three times three
They cheered her moving beauty in, and she
Came to her berth so noble, so superb;
Swayed like a queen, and answered to the curb.

Then in the sunset's flush they went aloft,
And unbent sails in that most lovely hour
When the light gentles and the wind is soft,
And beauty in the heart breaks like a flower.
Working aloft they saw the mountain tower,
Snow to the peak; they heard the launchmen shout;
And bright along the bay the lights came out.

And then the night fell dark, and all night long
The pointed mountain pointed at the stars,
Frozen, alert, austere; the eagle's song
Screamed from her desolate screes and splintered scars.
On her intense crags where the air is sparse
The stars looked down; their many golden eyes
Watched her and burned, burned out, and came to rise.

Silent the finger of the summit stood,
Icy in pure, thin air, glittering with snows.
Then the sun's coming turned the peak to blood,
And in the rest-house the muleteers arose.
And all day long, where only the eagle goes,
Stones, loosened by the sun, fall; the stones falling
Fill empty gorge on gorge with echoes calling.

GLOSSARY

EXPLANATIONS OF SOME OF THE SEA
TERMS USED IN THE POEM

BACKSTAYS: wire ropes which support the masts against lateral and after strains.

BARNEY'S BULL: a figure in marine proverb. A jewel in marine repartee.

BELLS: two bells (one forward, one aft), which are struck every half-hour in a certain manner to mark the passage of the watches.

BITTS: strong wooden structures (built round each mast) upon which running rigging is secured.

BLOCK: a sheaved pulley.

BOATSWAIN: a supernumerary or idler, generally attached to the mate's watch, and holding considerable authority over the crew.

BOUILLI TIN: any tin that contains, or has contained, preserved meat.

BOWS: the forward extremity of a ship.

BRACE-BLOCKS: pulleys through which the braces travel.

BRACES: ropes by which the yards are inclined forward or aft.

BUMBOAT PAN: soft bread sold by the bumboat man, a kind of sea costermonger who trades with ships in port.

BUNT: those cloths of a square sail which are nearest to the mast when the sail is set. The central portion of a furled square sail. The human abdomen (figuratively).

BUNTLINES: ropes which help to confine square sails to the yards in the operation of furling.

CHOCKS: wooden stands on which the boats rest.

CLEATS: iron or wooden contrivances to which ropes may be secured.

CLEW-LINES: ropes by which the lower corners of square sails are lifted.

CLEWS: the lower corners of square sails.

CLIPPER: a title of honour given to ships of more than usual speed and beauty.

COAMING: the raised rim of a hatchway; a barrier at a doorway to keep water from entering.

COURSES: the large square sails set upon the lower yards of sailing ships. The mizen course is called the 'crojick'.

CRINGLED: fitted with iron rings or cringles, many of which are let into sails or sail-roping for various purposes.

CROJICK OR CROSS-JACK: a square sail set upon the lower yard of the mizen-mast.

DUNGAREES: thin blue or khaki-coloured overalls made from coconut fibre.

FAIRLEADS: rings of wood or iron by means of which running rigging is led in any direction.

FIFE-RAILS: strong wooden shelves fitted with iron pins, to which ropes may be secured.

FISH-HOOKS: i.e., fingers.

FOOT-ROPES: ropes on which men stand when working aloft.

FO'C'S'LE: the cabin or cabins in which the men are berthed. It is usually an iron deck-house divided through the middle into two compartments for the two watches, and fitted with wooden bunks. Sometimes it is even fitted with lockers and an iron water-tank.

FOXES: strands, yarns, or arrangements of yarns of rope.

FRAP: to wrap round with rope.

FREEING-PORTS: iron doors in the ship's side which open outwards to free the decks of water.

FUTTOCK-SHROUDS: iron bars to which the topmast rigging is secured. As they project outward and upward from the masts they are difficult to clamber over.

GALLEY: the ship's kitchen.

GANTLINE (GIRTLINE): a rope used for the sending of sails up and down from aloft.

GASKETS: ropes by which the sails are secured in furling.

HALF-DECK: a cabin or apartment in which the apprentices are berthed. Its situation is usually the ship's waist, but it is sometimes further aft, and occasionally it is under the poop or even right forward under the top-gallant fo'c's'le.

HALLIARDS: ropes by which sails are hoisted.

HARNESS-ROOM: an office or room from which the salt meat is issued, and in which it is sometimes stored.

HAWSE: the bows or forward end of a ship.

HEAD: the forward part of a ship. That upper edge of a square sail which is attached to the yard.

HOUSE-FLAG: the special flag of the firm to which a ship belongs.

IDLERS: the members of the round-house mess, generally consisting of the carpenter, cook, sailmaker, boatswain, painter, etc., are known as the idlers.

JACK or JACKSTAY: an iron bar (fitted along all yards in sailing ships) to which the head of a square sail is secured when bent.

KITES: light upper sails.

LEECHES: the outer edges of square sails. In furling some square sails the leech is dragged inwards till it lies level with the head upon the surface of the yard. This is done by the first man who gets upon the yard, beginning at the weather side.

LOGSHIP: a contrivance by which a ship's speed is measured.

LOWER TOPSAIL: the second sail from the deck on square-rigged masts. It is a very strong, important sail.

MARLINE: tarry line or coarse string made of rope-yarns twisted together.

MATE: the First or Chief Mate is generally called the Mate.

MIZEN-TOPMAST-HEAD: the summit of the second of the three or four spars which make the complete mizen-mast.

MUDHOOKS: anchors.

PINS: iron or wooden bars to which running rigging is secured.

POINTING: a kind of neat plait with which ropes are sometimes ended off or decorated.

POOP-BREAK: the forward end of the after superstructure.

RATLINES: the rope steps placed across the shrouds to enable the seamen to go aloft.

REEFERS: apprentices.

REEF-POINTS: ropes by which the area of some sails may be reduced in the operation of reefing. Reef-points are securely fixed to the sails fitted with them, and when not in use their ends patter continually upon the canvas with a gentle drumming noise.

REEL: a part of the machinery used with a logship.

ROUND-HOUSE: a cabin (of all shapes except round) in which the idlers are berthed.

ROYALS: light upper square sails; the fourth, fifth, or sixth sails from the deck according to the mast's rig.

SAIL-ROOM: a large room or compartment in which the ship's sails are stored.

'SAILS': the sailmaker is meant.

SCUTTLE-BUTT: a cask containing fresh water.

SHACKLES: rope handles for a sea-chest.

SHEET-BLOCKS: iron blocks, by means of which sails are sheeted home. In any violent wind they beat upon the mast with great rapidity and force.

SHEETS: ropes or chains which extend the lower corners of square sails in the operation of sheeting home.

SHIFTING SUITS (OF SAILS): the operation of removing a ship's sails and replacing them with others.

SHROUDS: wire ropes of great strength, which support lateral strains on masts.

SHROUD-SCREWS: iron contrivances by which shrouds are hove taut.

SIDELIGHTS: a sailing ship carries two of these between sunset and sunrise: one green, to starboard; one red, to port.

SIGHTS: observations to help in the finding of a ship's position.

SKID: a wooden contrivance on which ship's boats rest.

SKYSAILS: the uppermost square sails; the fifth, sixth, or seventh sails from the deck according to the mast's rig.

SLATTING: the noise made by sails flogging in the wind.

SLUSH: grease, melted fat.

SOUTH-WESTER: a kind of oilskin hat. A gale from the south-west.

SPIT BROWN: to chew tobacco.

SQUARE SENNIT: a cunning plait which makes a four-square bar.

STAYSAILS: fore and aft sails set upon the stays between the masts.

STOW: to furl.

STROP (the, putting on): a strop is a grummet or rope ring. The two players kneel down facing each other, the strop is placed over their heads, and the men then try to pull each other over by the strength of their neck-muscles.

SWING PORTS: iron doors in the ship's side which open outwards to free the decks from water.

TACKLE (pronounced 'taykel'): blocks, ropes, pulleys, etc.

TAKE A CAULK: to sleep upon the deck.

TOPSAILS: the second and third sails from the deck on the masts of a modern square-rigged ship are known as the lower and upper topsails.

TRUCKS: the summits of the masts.

UPPER TOPSAIL: the third square sail from the deck on the masts of square-rigged ships.

YARDS: the steel or wooden spars (placed across masts) from which square sails are set.

Reynard the Fox

OR

The Ghost Heath Run

INTRODUCTION

THE STORY *Reynard the Fox* was written in the year 1919 at Boars Hill, in Berkshire.

As a child, living within half a mile of a kennel of fox-hounds, I had often seen both hounds and huntsmen. As a boy I had sometimes followed hounds on foot from a meet to a covert, had seen the fox away, and (now and then) had judged the chances and seen rather more. But when wishing to write of a fox-hunt, this scanty and remote knowledge did not serve. I knew that I knew nothing about it, and set myself to learn from the many books that exist upon the matter, and from a few friends to whom hunting was the breath of life.

It had been a part of my design to show the characters composing an English country society (such as had existed before the War) all together at once. As far as my knowledge went, this much mixed society could be seen all together only at a fox-hunt. At the time of my writing, this country society had already much changed from what I had seen and known as a child.

My knowledge of foxes was of the slightest, for foxes are shy, night-moving animals. I had seen (I believe) only two or three un-hunted foxes in all my life. Soon after I had begun to write the story, I was made to feel, in a strange and happy way, that something not before known to me, some Sympathy, something (shall we say?) akin to the Tutelary Spirit of Foxes, was there to help. Soon, when I wished to see a Fox close-to, I found a beautiful dog-fox, still warm, dead (I feel sure from poison) at a Berkshire pond-side. A week or two later, a vixen laid-up her cubs in my garden; and a little later, a poor fox caught in a gin-trap knew me for a friend and let me release him, without giving me the expected bite.

But though a hunted fox was my subject, it was but the image of my subject. For more than four years before I wrote, something primitive, wild, beautiful and strange in the Spirit of Man had been pursued through most of Europe with the threat of death. It had survived the chase, but as a hunted fox may survive a long run, to lie panting somewhere till the heart stops beating. It was my hope that my Fox's heart should not stop beating.

JOHN MASEFIELD

PART I

THE meet was at 'The Cock and Pye
By Charles and Martha Enderby,'
The grey, three-hundred-year-old inn
Long since the haunt of Benjamin
The highwayman, who rode the bay.
The tavern fronts the coaching way,
The mail changed horses there of old.
It has a strip of grassy mould
In front of it, a broad green strip.
A trough, where horses' muzzles dip,
Stands opposite the tavern front,
And there that morning came the hunt,
To fill that quiet width of road
As full of men as Framilode
Is full of sea when tide is in.

The stables were alive with din
From dawn until the time of meeting.
A pad-groom gave a cloth a beating,
Knocking the dust out with a stake.
Two men cleaned stalls with fork and rake,
And one went whistling to the pump,
The handle whined, ker-lump, ker-lump,
The water splashed into the pail,
And, as he went, it left a trail,

Lipped over on the yard's bricked paving.
Two grooms (sent on before) were shaving
There in the yard, at glasses propped
On jutting bricks; they scraped and stropped,
And felt their chins and leaned and peered,
A woodland day was what they feared
(As second horseman), shaving there.
Then, in the stalls where hunters were,
Straw rustled as the horses shifted,
The hayseeds ticked and haystraws drifted
From racks as horses tugged their feed.
Slow gulping sounds of steady greed
Came from each stall, and sometimes stampings,
Whinnies (at well-known steps) and rampings,
To see the horse in the next stall.

Outside, the spangled cock did call
To scattering grain that Martha flung.
And many a time a mop was wrung
By Susan ere the floor was clean.
The harness-room, that busy scene,
Clinked and chinked from ostler's brightening
Rings and bits with dips of whitening,
Rubbing fox-flecks out of stirrups,
Dumbing buckles of their chirrups
By the touch of oily feathers.
Some, with stag's bones rubbed at leathers,
Brushed at saddle-flaps or hove
Saddle-linings to the stove.
Blue smoke from strong tobacco drifted
Out of the yard, the passers snifft it,
Mixed with the strong ammonia flavour
Of horses' stables and the savour

Of saddle-paste and polish spirit
Which put the gleam on flap and tirrit.
The grooms in shirts with rolled-up sleeves,
Belted by girths of coloured weaves,
Groomed the clipped hunters in their stalls.
One said: 'My dad cured saddle-galls,
He called it Dr Barton's cure—
Hog's lard and borax, laid on pure.'
And others said: 'Ge' back, my son.'
'Stand over, girl; now, girl, ha'done.'
'Now, boy, no snapping; gently. Crikes!
He gives a rare pinch when he likes.'
'Drawn blood? I thought he looked a biter.'
'I give 'em all sweet spit of nitre
For that, myself: that sometimes cures.'
'Now, Beauty, mind them feet of yours.'
They groomed, and sissed with hissing notes
To keep the dust out of their throats.

*   *   *

There came again and yet again
The feed-box lid, the swish of grain,
Or Joe's boots stamping in the loft,
The hay-fork's stab and then the soft
Hay's scratching slither down the shoot.
Then with a thud some horse's foot
Stamped, and the gulping munch again
Resumed its lippings at the grain.

*   *   *

The road outside the inn was quiet
Save for the poor, mad, restless pyat
Hopping his hanging wicker-cage.
No calmative of sleep or sage

Will cure the fever to be free.
He shook the wicker ceaselessly
Now up, now down, but never out,
On wind-waves, being blown about,
Looking for dead things good to eat.
His cage was strewn with scattered wheat.

*   *   *

At ten o'clock, the Doctor's lad
Brought up his master's hunting pad
And put him in a stall, and leaned
Against the stall, and sissed, and cleaned
The port and cannons of his curb.
He chewed a sprig of smelling herb.
He sometimes stopped, and spat, and chid
The silly things his master did.

*   *   *

At twenty past, old Baldock strode
His ploughman's straddle down the road.
An old man with a gaunt, burnt face,
His eyes rapt back on some far place
Like some starved, half-mad saint in bliss
In God's world through the rags of this.
He leaned upon a stake of ash
Cut from a sapling: many a gash
Was in his old, full-skirted coat.
The twisted muscles in his throat
Moved, as he swallowed, like taut cord.
His oaken face was seamed and gored;
He halted by the inn and stared
On that far bliss, that place prepared,
Beyond his eyes, beyond his mind.

*   *   *

Then Thomas Copp, of Cowfoot's Wynd,
Drove up; and stopped to take a glass.
'I hope they'll gallop on my grass,'
He said; 'my little girl does sing
To see the red coats galloping.
It's good for grass, too, to be trodden
Except they poach it, where it's sodden.'

   ★   ★   ★

Then Billy Waldrist, from the Lynn,
With Jockey Hill, from Pitts, came in
And had a sip of gin and stout
To help the jockey's sweatings out.
'Rare day for scent,' the jockey said.

A pony like a feather bed
On four short sticks, took place aside.
The little girl who rode astride
Watched everything with eyes that glowed
With glory in the horse she rode.

   ★   ★   ★

At half-past ten some lads on foot
Came to be beaters to a shoot
Of rabbits on the Warren Hill.
Rough sticks they had, and Hob and Jill,
Their ferrets, in a bag, and netting.
They talked of dinner-beer and betting,
And jeered at those who stood around.
They rolled their dogs upon the ground,
And teased them: 'Rats,' they cried, 'go fetch!'
'Go seek, good Roxer; 'z bite, good betch.
What dinner-beer'll they give us, lad?
Sex quarts the lot last year we had.

They'd ought to give us seven this.
Seek, Susan; what a betch it is.'

*   *   *

A pommle cob came trotting up,
Round-bellied like a drinking-cup,
Bearing on back a pommle man,
Round-bellied like a drinking-can.
The clergyman from Condicote.
His face was scarlet from his trot,
His white hair bobbed about his head
As halos do round clergy dead.
He asked Tom Copp, 'How long to wait?'
His loose mouth opened like a gate,
To pass the wagons of his speech.
He had a mighty voice to preach,
Though indolent in other matters.
He let his children go in tatters.

*   *   *

His daughter Madge on foot, flush-cheeked
In broken hat and boots that leaked,
With bits of hay all over her,
Her plain face grinning at the stir
(A broad pale face, snub-nosed, with speckles
Of sandy eyebrows sprinkt with freckles),
Came after him and stood apart
Beside the darling of her heart,
Miss Hattie Dyce from Baydon Dean,
A big young fair one, chiselled clean
Brow, chin and nose, with great blue eyes
All innocence and sweet surprise,
And golden hair piled coil on coil,
Too beautiful for time to spoil.

They talked in undertones together—
Not of the hunting, nor the weather.

      *   *   *

Old Steven from Scratch Steven Place
(A white beard and a rosy face)
Came next on his stringhalty grey.
'I've come to see the hounds away,'
He said, 'and ride a field or two.
We old have better things to do
Than breaking all our necks for fun.'
He shone on people like the sun,
And on himself for shining so.

      *   *   *

Three men came riding in a row;
John Pym, a bull-man, quick to strike,
Gross and blunt-headed like a shrike,
Yet sweet-voiced as a piping flute;
Tom See, the trainer, from the Toot,
Red, with an angry, puzzled face
And mouth twitched upward out of place,
Sucking cheap grapes and spitting seeds;
And Stone, of Bartle's Cattle Feeds,
A man whose bulk of flesh and bone
Made people call him Twenty Stone.
He was the man who stood a pull
At Tencombe with the Jersey bull,
And brought the bull back to his stall.

      *   *   *

Some children ranged the tavern-wall,
Sucking their thumbs and staring hard;
Some grooms brought horses from the yard.
Jane Selbie said to Ellen Tranter,
'A lot on 'em come doggin', ant her?'

'A lot on 'em,' said Ellen. 'Look,
There'm Mr Gaunt of Water's Hook.
They say he . . .' (whispered). 'Law!' said Jane.
Gaunt flung his heel across the mane,
And slithered from his horse and stamped.
'Boots tight,' he said, 'my feet are cramped.'

A loose-shod horse came clicking-clack;
Nick Wolvesey on a hired hack
Came tittup, like a cup and ball.
One saw the sun, moon, stars, and all
The great green earth 'twixt him and saddle;
Then Molly Wolvesey riding straddle,
Red as a rose with eyes like sparks;
Two boys from college out for larks
Hunted bright Molly for a smile,
But were not worth their quarry's while.

　　　　　*　　　*　　　*

Two eye-glassed gunners dressed in tweed
Came with a spaniel on a lead
And waited for a fellow-gunner.

The parson's son, the famous runner,
Came dressed to follow hounds on foot.
His knees were red as yew-tree root
From being bare, day in, day out.
He wore a blazer, and a clout
(His sweater's arms) tied round his neck.
His football shorts had many a speck
And splash of mud from many a fall
Got as he picked the slippery ball
Heeled out behind a breaking scrum.
He grinned at people, but was dumb,

Not like these lousy foreigners.
The otter-hounds and harriers
From Godstow to the Wye all knew him.

And with him came the stock which grew him,
The parson and his sporting wife.
She was a stout one, full of life,
With red, quick, kindly, manly face.
She held the knave, queen, king and ace.
In every hand she played with men.
She was no sister to the hen,
But fierce and minded to be queen.
She wore a coat and skirt of green,
A waistcoat cut of hunting red,
Her tiepin was a fox's head.

The parson was a manly one,
His jolly eyes were bright with fun
His jolly mouth was well inclined
To cry aloud his jolly mind
To everyone, in jolly terms.
He did not talk of churchyard worms,
But of our privilege as dust
To box a lively bout with lust
Ere going to heaven to rejoice.
He loved the sound of his own voice,
His talk was like a charge of horse,
His build was all compact, for force,
Well-knit, well-made, well-coloured, eager.
He kept no Lent to make him meagre,
He loved his God, himself and man,
He never said, 'Life's wretched span;

This wicked world,' in any sermon.
This body that we feed the worm on,
To him, was jovial stuff that thrilled.
He liked to see the foxes killed;
But most he felt himself in clover
To hear, 'Hen left, hare right, cock over,'
At woodside, when the leaves are brown.
Some grey cathedral in a town
Where drowsy bells toll out the time
To shaven closes sweet with lime,
And wallflower roots rive out the mortar
All summer on the Norman dortar
Was certain some day to be his;
Nor would a mitre go amiss
To him, because he governed well.
His voice was like the tenor bell
When services were said and sung,
And he had read in many a tongue,
Arabic, Hebrew, Spanish, Greek.

     *   *   *

Two bright young women, nothing meek,
Rode up on bicycles and propped
Their wheels in such wise that they dropped
To bring the parson's son to aid.
Their cycling suits were tailor-made,
Smart, mannish, pert, but feminine.
The colour and the zest of wine
Were in their presence and their bearing;
Like spring, they brought the thought of pairing,
The parson's lady thought them pert.
And they could mock a man and flirt,
Do billiard tricks with corks and pennies,
Sing ragtime songs and win at tennis

The silver cigarette-case prize.
They had good colour and bright eyes,
Bright hair, bright teeth and pretty skin,
Which many lads had longed to win
On darkened stairways after dances.
Their reading was the last romances,
And they were dashing hockey players.
Men called them 'Jill and Joan, the slayers.'
They were as bright as fresh sweet-peas.

Old Farmer Bennett followed these
Upon his big-boned savage black,
Whose mule-teeth yellowed to bite back
Whatever came within his reach.
Old Bennett sat him like a leech,
The grim old rider seemed to be
As hard about the mouth as he.

       *   *   *

The beaters nudged each other's ribs
With 'There he goes, his bloody Nibs.
He come on Joe and Anty Cop
And beat 'em with his hunting-crop
Like tho' they'd bin a sack of beans.
His pickers were a pack of queans,
And Joe and Anty took a couple.
He caught 'em there, and banged 'em supple.
Women and men, he didn't care
(He'd kill 'em some day, if he dare),
He beat the whole four nearly dead:
"I'll learn 'ee rabbit in my shed;
That's how my ricks get set afire."
That's what he said, the bloody liar;

Old oaf! I'd like to burn his ricks,
Th' old swine's too free with fists and sticks.
He keeps that Mrs Jones himselve.'

*   *   *

Just like an axehead on its helve
Old Bennett sat and watched the gathering.
He'd given many a man a lathering
In field or barn, and women too.
His cold eye reached the women through
With comment, and the men with scorn.
He hated women gently born,
He hated all beyond his grasp,
For he was minded like the asp,
That strikes whatever is not dust.

*   *   *

Charles Copse, of Copse Hold Manor, thrust
Next into view. In face and limb
The beauty and the grace of him
Were like the Golden Age returned.
His grave eyes steadily discerned
The good in men and what was wise.
He had deep blue, mild-coloured eyes
And shocks of harvest-coloured hair
Still beautiful with youth. An air
Or power of kindness went about him;
No heart of youth could ever doubt him
Or fail to follow where he led.
He was a genius, simply bred,
And quite unconscious of his power.
He was the very red rose flower
Of all that coloured countryside.
Gauchos had taught him how to ride.

He knew all arts, but practised most
The art of bettering flesh and ghost
In men and lads down in the mud.
He knew no class in flesh and blood.
He loved his kind. He spent some pith,
Long since, relieving Ladysmith.
Many a horse he trotted tame
Heading commandos from their aim
In those old days upon the veldt.

    ★   ★   ★

An old bear in a scarlet pelt
Came next, old Squire Harridew,
His eyebrows gave a man the grue,
So bushy and so fierce they were;
He had a bitter tongue to swear.
A fierce, hot, hard, old, stupid squire,
With all his liver made of fire,
Small brain, great courage, mulish will.
The hearts in all his house stood still
When someone crossed the Squire's path.
For he was terrible in wrath,
And smashed whatever came to hand.
Two things he failed to understand,
The foreigner and what was new.

His daughters, Carrie, Jane and Lou,
Rode with him, Carrie at his side.
His son, the ne'er-do-weel, had died
In Arizona long before.
The Squire set the greatest store
By Carrie, youngest of the three,
And lovely to the blood was she;
D.—7

Blonde, with a face of blush and cream,
And eyes deep violet in their gleam,
Bright blue when quiet in repose,
She was a very golden rose.
And many a man when sunset came
Would see the manor windows flame,
And think, 'My beauty's home is there.'
Queen Helen had less golden hair,
Queen Cleopatra paler lips,
Queen Blanche's eyes were in eclipse
By golden Carrie's glancing by.
She had a wit for mockery
And sang mild, pretty, senseless songs
Of sunsets, Heav'n and lovers' wrongs,
Sweet to the Squire when he had dined.
A rosebud need not have a mind.
A lily is not sweet from learning.

*   *   *

Jane looked like a dark-lantern, burning,
Outwardly dark, unkempt, uncouth,
But minded like the living truth,
A friend that nothing shook nor wearied.
She was not 'Darling Jane'd' nor 'Dearie'd'.
She was all prickles to the touch,
So sharp that many feared to clutch,
So keen that many thought her bitter.
She let the little sparrows twitter.
She had a hard, ungracious way.
Her storm of hair was iron-grey,
And she was passionate in her heart
For women's souls that burn apart,
Just as her mother's had, with Squire.

She gave the sense of smouldering fire.
She was not happy being a maid,
At home, with Squire, but she stayed,
Enduring life, however bleak,
To guard her sisters, who were weak,
And force a life for them from Squire.
And she had roused and stood his fire
A hundred times, and earned his hate,
To win those two a better state.
Long years before the Canon's son
Had cared for her, but he had gone
To Klondyke, to the mines, for gold,
To find, in some strange way untold,
A foreign grave that no men knew.

    ★   ★   ★

No depth, nor beauty, was in Lou,
But charm and fun, for she was merry,
Round, sweet and little, like a cherry,
With laughter like a robin's singing;
She was not kitten-like and clinging,
But pert and arch and fond of flirting,
In mocking ways that were not hurting,
And merry ways that women pardoned.
Not being married yet she gardened.
She loved sweet music; she would sing
Songs made before the German King
Made England German in her mind.
She sang 'My Lady is unkind',
'The Hunt is up', and those sweet things
Which Thomas Campion set to strings,
'Thrice toss', and 'What', and 'Where are now?'

    ★   ★   ★

The next to come was Major Howe
Driv'n in a dog-cart by a groom.
The testy major was in fume
To find no hunter standing waiting;
The groom who drove him caught a rating,
The groom who had the horse in stable
Was damned in half the tongues of Babel,
The Major being hot and heady
When horse or dinner was not ready.
He was a lean, tough, liverish fellow,
With pale blue eyes (the whites pale yellow),
Moustache clipped toothbrush-wise, and jaws
Shaved bluish like old partridge claws.
When he had stripped his coat he made
A speckless presence for parade,
New pink, white cords, and glossy tops,
New gloves, the newest thing in crops,
Worn with an air that well expressed
His sense that no one else was dressed.

      ★   ★   ★

Quick trotting after Major Howe
Came Doctor Frome of Quickemshow,
A smiling silent man whose brain
Knew all of every secret pain
In every man and woman there.
Their inmost lives were all laid bare
To him, because he touched their lives
When strong emotions sharp as knives
Brought out what sort of soul each was.
As secret as the graveyard grass
He was, as he had need to be.
At some time he had had to see

Each person there, sans clothes, sans mask,
Sans lying even, when to ask
Probed a tamed spirit into truth.

       ★   ★   ★

Richard, his son, a jolly youth,
Rode with him, fresh from Thomas's,
As merry as a yearling is
In May-time in a clover patch.
He was a gallant chick to hatch,
Big, brown and smiling, blithe and kind,
With all his father's love of mind
And greater force to give it act.
To see him when the scrum was packed,
Heave, playing forward, was a sight.
His tackling was the crowd's delight
In many a danger close to goal.
The pride in the three-quarter's soul
Dropped, like a wet rag, when he collared.
He was as steady as a bollard,
And gallant as a skysail yard,
He rode a chestnut mare which sparred.
In good St Thomas' Hospital
He was the crown imperial
Of all the scholars of his year.

       ★   ★   ★

The Harold lads, from Tencombe Weir,
Came all on foot in corduroys,
Poor widowed Mrs Harold's boys,
Dick, Hal and Charles, whose father died.
(Will Masemore shot him in the side
By accident at Masemore Farm.
A hazel knocked Will Masemore's arm

In getting through a hedge; his gun
Was not half-cocked, so it was done,
And those three boys left fatherless.)
Their gaitered legs were in a mess
With good red mud from twenty ditches,
Hal's face was plastered like his breeches.
Dick chewed a twig of juniper.
They kept at distance from the stir,
Their loss had made them lads apart.

*   *   *

Next came the Colways' pony-cart
From Coln St Evelyn's with the party.
Hugh Colway, jovial, bold and hearty,
And Polly Colway's brother, John
(Their horses had been both sent on),
And Polly Colway drove them there.
Poor pretty Polly Colway's hair!
The grey mare killed her at the brook
Down seven springs mead at Water Hook
Just one month later, poor sweet woman.
Her brother was a rat-faced Roman,
Lean, puckered, tight-skinned from the sea,
Commander in the *Canace*,
Able to drive a horse, or ship,
Or crew of men without a whip
By will, as long as they could go.
His face would wrinkle, row on row,
From mouth to hair-roots when he laughed,
He looked ahead as though his craft
Were with him still, in dangerous channels.
He and Hugh Colway tossed their flannels
Into the pony-cart and mounted.
Six foiled attempts the watchers counted,

The horses being bickering things
That so much scarlet made like kings,
Such sidling and such pawing and shifting.

*　　　*　　　*

When Hugh was up his mare went drifting
Sidelong and feeling with her heels
For horses' legs and poshay wheels,
While lather creamed her neat clipped skin.
Hugh guessed her foibles with a grin.
He was a rich town-merchant's son,
A wise and kind man, fond of fun,
Who loved to have a troop of friends
At Coln St Eves for all week-ends,
And troops of children in for tea.
He gloried in a Christmas-tree.
And Polly was his heart's best treasure,
And Polly was a golden pleasure
To everyone, to see or hear.

*　　　*　　　*

Poor Polly's dying struck him queer,
He was a darkened man thereafter,
Cowed, silent, he would wince at laughter
And be so gentle it was strange
Even to see. Life loves to change.

*　　　*　　　*

Now Coln St Evelyn's hearths are cold,
The shutters up, the hunters sold,
And green mould damps the locked front door,
But this was still a month before,
And Polly, golden in the chaise,
Still smiled, and there were golden days,
Still thirty days, for those dear lovers.

*　　　*　　　*

The Riddens came, from Ocle Covers,
Bill Ridden riding Stormalong
(By Tempest out of Love-me-Long),
A proper handful of a horse
That nothing but the Aintree course
Could bring to terms, save Bill perhaps.
All sport, from bloody war to scraps,
Came well to Bill, that big-mouthed smiler.
They nicknamed him 'the mug-beguiler',
For Billy lived too much with horses,
In copers' yards and sharpers' courses,
To lack the sharper-coper streak.
He did not turn the other cheek
When struck (as English Christians do);
He boxed like a Whitechapel Jew,
And many a time his knuckles bled
Against a racecourse-gipsy's head.
For 'hit him first and argue later'
Was truth at Billy's Alma Mater,
Not love, not any bosh of love.
His hand was like a chamois glove,
And riding was his chief delight.
He bred the chaser Chinese-White
From Lilybud by Mandarin.
And when his mouth tucked corners in,
And scent was high and hounds were going,
He went across a field like snowing
And tackled anything that came.

*   *   *

His wife, Sal Ridden, was the same,
A loud, bold, blonde, abundant mare
With white horse-teeth and stooks of hair

(Like polished brass) and such a manner
It flaunted from her like a banner.
Her father was Tom See the trainer.
She rode a lovely earth-disdainer
Which she and Billy wished to sell.

*   *   *

Behind them rode her daughter Belle,
A strange, shy, lovely girl, whose face
Was sweet with thought and proud with race,
And bright with joy at riding there.
She was as good as blowing air,
But shy and difficult to know.
The kittens in the barley-mow,
The setter's toothless puppies sprawling,
The blackbird in the apple calling,
All knew her spirit more than we.
So delicate these maidens be
In loving lovely helpless things.

The Manor set, from Tencombe Rings,
Came with two friends, a set of six.
Ed Manor with his cockerel chicks,
Nob, Cob and Bunny, as they called them
(God help the school or rule which galled them;
They carried head), and friends from town.
Ed Manor trained on Tencombe Down.
He once had been a famous bat;
He had that stroke, 'the Manor-pat',
Which snicked the ball for three, past cover.
He once scored twenty in an over.
But now he cricketed no more.
He purpled in the face and swore

At all three sons, and trained, and told
Long tales of cricketing of old,
When he alone had saved his side,
Drink made it doubtful if he lied.
Drink purpled him, he could not face
The fences now, nor go the pace
He brought his friends to meet; no more.

*   *   *

His big son Nob, at whom he swore,
Swore back at him, for Nob was surly,
Tall, shifty, sullen-smiling, burly,
Quite fearless, built with such a jaw
That no man's rule could be his law
Nor any woman's son his master.
Boxing he relished. He could plaster
All those who boxed out Tencombe way.
A front tooth had been knocked away
Two days before, which put his mouth
A little to the east of south,
And put a venom in his laughter.

*   *   *

Cob was a lighter lad, but dafter,
Just past eighteen, while Nob was twenty,
Nob had no nerves but Cob had plenty,
So Cobby went where Nobby led.
He had no brains inside his head,
Was fearless, just like Nob, but put
Some clog of folly round his foot,
Where Nob put will of force or fraud.
He spat aside and muttered Gawd
When vext; he took to whisky kindly

And loved and followed Nobby blindly,
And rode as in the saddle born.

*   *   *

Bun looked upon the two with scorn.
He was the youngest, and was wise.
He too was fair, with sullen eyes,
He too (a year before) had had
A zest for going to the bad,
With Cob and Nob. He knew the joys
Of drinking with the stable-boys,
Or smoking while he filled his skin
With pints of Guinness dashed with gin
And Cobby yelled a bawdy ditty,
Or cutting Nobby for the kitty,
And damning people's eyes and guts,
Or drawing evening-church for sluts;
He knew them all and now was quit.

*   *   *

Sweet Polly Colway managed it
And Bunny changed. He dropped his drink
(The pleasant pit's seductive brink),
He started working in the stable,
And well, for he was shrewd and able.
He left the doubtful female friends
Picked up at Evening-Service ends,
He gave up cards and swore no more.
Nob called him 'the Reforming Whore',
'The Soul's Awakening', or 'The Text',
Nob being always coarse when vexed.

*   *   *

Ed Manor's friends were Hawke and Sladd,
Old college friends, the last he had,
Rare horsemen, but their nerves were shaken
By all the whisky they had taken.
Hawke's hand was trembling on his rein.
His eyes were dead-blue like a vein,
His peaked, sad face was touched with breeding,
His querulous mind was quaint from reading,
His piping voice still quirked with fun.
Many a mad thing he had done,
Riding to hounds and going to races.
A glimmer of the gambler's graces,
Wit, courage, devil, touched his talk.

*   *   *

Sladd's big fat face was white as chalk,
His mind went wandering, swift yet solemn,
Twixt winning post and betting-column,
The weights and forms and likely colts.
He said, 'This road is full of jolts.
I shall be seasick riding here.
Oh, damn last night with that liqueur!'

Len Stokes rode up on Peterkin;
He owned the downs by Baydon Whin;
And grazed some thousand sheep; the boy
Grinned round at men with jolly joy
At being alive and being there.
His big round face and mop of hair
Shone, his great teeth shone in his grin.
The clean blood in his clear tanned skin
Ran merry, and his great voice mocked
His young friends present till they rocked.

*   *   *

Steer Harpit came from Rowell Hill,
A small, frail man, all heart and will,
A sailor, as his voice betrayed.
He let his whip-thong droop and played
At snicking off the grass-blades with it.
John Hankerton, from Compton Lythitt,
Was there with Pity Hankerton,
And Mike, their good-for-little son,
Back, smiling, from his seventh job.
Joan Urch was there upon her cob,
Tom Sparsholt on his lanky grey,
John Restrop from Hope Goneaway,
And Vaughan, the big black handsome devil,
Loose-lipped with song and wine and revel,
All rosy from his morning tub.

*   *   *

The Godsdown tigress with her cub
(Lady and Tommy Crowmarsh) came.
The great eyes smouldered in the dame,
Wit glittered, too, which few men saw.
There was more beauty there than claw.
Tommy in bearing, horse and dress,
Was black, fastidious handsomeness,
Choice to his trimmed soul's finger-tips,
Heredia's sonnets on his lips.
A line undrawn, a plate not bitten,
A stone uncut, a phrase unwritten
That would be perfect, made his mind.
A choice pull from a rare print, signed,
Was Tommy. He collected plate
(Old Sheffield), and he owned each state
Of all the Meryon Paris etchings.
Colonel Sir Button Budd of Fletchings

Was there; Long Robert Thrupp was there
(Three yards of him men said there were),
Long as the King of Prussia's fancy.
He rode the long-legged Necromancy,
A useless racehorse that could canter.
George Childrey with his jolly banter
Was there, Nick Childrey, too, come down
The night before from London town
To hunt and have his lungs blown clean.
The Ilsley set from Tuttocks Green
Was there (old Henry Ilsley drove).
Carlotta Ilsley brought her love,
A flop-jowled broker from the city.
Men pitied her, for she was pretty.

       *   *   *

Some grooms and second horsemen mustered.
A lot of men on foot were clustered
Round the inn-door all busy drinking,
One heard the kissing glasses clinking
In passage as the tray was brought.
Two terriers (which they had there) fought
There on the green, a loud, wild whirl.
Bell stopped them like a gallant girl.
The hens behind the tavern clucked.

Then on a horse which bit and bucked
(The half-broke four-year-old Marauder)
Came Minton-Price of th' Afghan border,
Lean, puckered, yellowed, knotted, scarred,
Tough as a hide-rope twisted hard,
Tense tiger-sinew knit to bone.
Strange-wayed from having lived alone
With Kafir, Afghan and Beloosh,

In stations frozen in the Koosh
Where nothing but the bullet sings.
His mind had conquered many things—
Painting, mechanics, physics, law.
White-hot, hand-beaten things to draw
Self-hammered from his own soul's stithy.
His speech was blacksmith-sparked and pithy.
Danger had been his brother bred;
The stones had often been his bed
In bickers with the border-thieves.

*　　*　　*

A chestnut mare with swerves and heaves
Came plunging, scattered all the crowd,
She tossed her head and laughed aloud
And bickered sideways past the meet.
From pricking ears to mincing feet
She was all tense with blood and quiver,
You saw her clipt hide twitch and shiver
Over her netted cords of veins.
She carried Cothill, of the Sleins,
A tall, black, bright-eyed, handsome lad.
Great power and great grace he had.
Men hoped the greatest things of him.
His grace made people think him slim,
But he was muscled like a horse,
A sculptor would have wrought his torse
In bronze or marble for Apollo.
He loved to hurry like a swallow
For miles on miles of short-grassed sweet,
Blue, hare-belled downs where dewy feet
Of pure winds hurry ceaselessly.
He loved the downland like a sea.

The downland where the kestrels hover—
The downland had him for a lover.

            ★   ★   ★

And every other thing he loved
In which a clean free spirit moved.

            ★   ★   ★

So beautiful he was, so bright,
He looked to men like young delight
Gone courting April maidenhood,
That has the primrose in her blood,
He on his mincing lady mare.

            ★   ★   ★

Ock Gurney and old Pete were there
Riding their bonny cobs and swearing,
Ock's wife had giv'n them both a fairing,
A horse-rosette red, white and blue.
Their cheeks were brown as any brew,
And every comer to the meet
Said, 'Hello, Ock,' or 'Morning, Pete,
Be you a-going to a wedding?'
'Why, noa,' they said, 'we'm going a-bedding,
Now ben't us, uncle, ben't us, Ock?'

Pete Gurney was a lusty cock
Turned sixty-three, but bright and hale,
A dairy-farmer in the vale,
Much like a robin in the face,
Much character in little space,
With little eyes like burning coal;
His mouth was like a slit or hole
In leather that was seamed and lined.
He had the russet-apple mind

That betters as the weather worsen.
He was a manly English person,
Kind to the core, brave, merry, true.
One grief he had, a grief still new,
That former Parson joined with Squire
In putting down the Playing Quire
In church, and putting organ in.
'Ah, boys, that was a pious din,
That Quire was; a pious praise
The noise was that we used to raise,
I and my serpent, George with his'n,
On Easter Day in "He is risen",
Or blessed Christmas in "Venite".
And how the trombone came in mighty
In Alleluias from the heart!
Pious, for each man played his part,
Not like 'tis now.' Thus he, still sore
For changes forty years before
When all (that could) in time and tune
Blew trumpets to the newë moon.
He was a bachelor from choice.
He and his nephew farmed the Boyce
Prime pasture-land for thirty cows
Ock's wife, Selina Jane, kept house,
And jolly were the three together.

*   *   *

Ock had a face like summer weather,
A broad red sun, split by a smile.
He mopped his forehead all the while
And said 'By damn,' and 'Ben't us, Unk?'
His eyes were close and deeply sunk.
He cursed his hunter like a lover:
'Now blast your soul, my dear, give over.
D —8

Woa, now, my pretty, damn your eyes.'
Like Pete, he was of middle size,
Dean-oak-like, stuggy, strong in shoulder.
He stood a wrestle like a boulder,
He had a back for pitching hay.
His singing voice was like a bay.
In talk he had a sideways spit,
Each minute to refresh his wit.
He cracked Brazil-nuts with his teeth.
He challenged Cobbet of the Heath
(Weight-lifting champion) once, but lost.
Hunting was what he loved the most
Next to his wife and Uncle Pete.
With beer to drink and cheese to eat
And rain in May to fill the grasses,
This life was not a dream that passes
To Ock, but like the summer flower.

*   *   *

But now the clock had struck the hour,
And round the corner down the road
The bob-bob-bobbing serpent flowed
With three black knobs upon its spine,
Three bobbing black caps in a line.
A glimpse of scarlet at the gap
Showed underneath each bobbing cap,
And at the corner by the gate
One heard Tom Dansey give a rate:
'Hey, drop it, Jumper; have a care!'
There came a growl, half-rate, half-swear
A spitting crack, a tuneful whimper
And sweet religion entered Jumper.

*   *   *

There was a general turn of faces,
The men and horses shifted places,
And round the corner came the Hunt,
Those feathery things, the hounds, in front.
Intent, wise, dipping, trotting, straying,
Smiling at people, shoving, playing,
Nosing to children's faces, waving
Their feathery sterns, and all behaving,
One eye to Dansey on Maroon.
Their padding cat-feet beat a tune,
And though they trotted up so quiet
Their noses brought them news of riot,
Wild smells of things with living blood,
Hot smells, against the grippers good,
Of weasel, rabbit, cat and hare,
Whose feet had been before them there,
Whose taint still tingled every breath;
But Dansey on Maroon was death,
So, though their noses roved, their feet
Larked and trit-trotted to the meet.

★   ★   ★

Bill Tall and Ell and Mirtie Key
(Aged fourteen years between the three)
Were flooded by them at the bend,
They thought their little lives would end;
The grave, sweet eyes looked into theirs,
Cold noses came, and clean short hairs,
And tails all crumpled up like ferns,
A sea of moving heads and sterns,
All round them, brushing coat and dress,
One paused, expecting a caress.

The children shrank into each other,
Shut eyes, clutched tight, and shouted 'Mother!'
With mouths wide open, catching tears.

*   *   *

Sharp Mrs Tall allayed their fears,
'Err out the road, the dogs won't hurt 'ee.
There now, you've cried your faces dirty.
More cleaning up for me to do.
What? Cry at dogs, great lumps like you?'
She licked her handkerchief and smeared
Their faces where the dirt appeared.

*   *   *

The hunt trit-trotted to the meeting,
Tom Dansey touching cap to greeting,
Slow lifting crop-thong to the rim,
No hunter there got more from him
Except some brightening of the eye
He halted at the Cock and Pye,
The hounds drew round him on the green,
Arrogant, Daffodil and Queen,
Closest, but all in little space.
Some lolled their tongues, some made grimace,
Yawning, or tilting nose in quest,
All stood and looked about with zest,
They were uneasy as they waited.
Their sires and dams had been well-mated,
They were a lovely pack for looks;
Their forelegs drumsticked without crooks,
Straight, without over-tread or bend,
Muscled to gallop to the end,
With neat feet round as any cat's.
Great-chested, muscled in the slats,

Bright, clean, short-coated, broad in shoulder,
With stag-like eyes that seemed to smoulder.
The heads well-cocked, the clean necks strong,
Brows broad, ears close, the muzzles long,
And all like racers in the thighs;
Their noses exquisitely wise,
Their minds being memories of smells;
Their voices like a ring of bells;
Their sterns all spirit, cock and feather;
Their colours like the English weather,
Magpie and hare, and badger-pye,
Like minglings in a double dye,
Some smutty-nosed, some tan, none bald;
Their manners were to come when called,
Their flesh was sinew knit to bone,
Their courage like a banner blown.
Their joy to push him out of cover,
And hunt him till they rolled him over.
They were as game as Robert Dover.

*   *   *

Tom Dansey was a famous whip,
Trained as a child in horsemanship,
Entered, as soon as he was able,
As boy at Caunter's racing-stable;
There, like the other boys, he slept
In stall beside the horse he kept,
Snug in the straw; and Caunter's stick
Brought morning to him all too quick.
He learned the high, quick gingery ways
Of thoroughbreds; his stable days
Made him a rider, groom and vet.
He promised to be too thick-set

For jockeying, so left it soon.
Now he was whip and rode Maroon.
He was a small, lean, wiry man,
With sunk cheeks weathered to a tan
Scarred by the spikes of hawthorn sprays
Dashed thro' head down, on going days,
In haste to see the line they took.
There was a beauty in his look,
It was intent. His speech was plain.
Maroon's head, reaching to the rein,
Had half his thought before he spoke.
His 'Gone away!' when foxes broke
Was like a bell. His chief delight
Was hunting fox from noon to night.
His pleasure lay in hounds and horses;
He loved the Seven Springs water-courses,
Those flashing brooks (in good sound grass,
Where scent would hang like breath on glass).
He loved the English countryside:
The wine-leaved bramble in the ride,
The lichen on the apple-trees,
The poultry ranging on the lees,
The farms, the moist earth-smelling cover,
His wife's green grave at Mitcheldover,
Where snowdrops pushed at the first thaw.
Under his hide his heart was raw
With joy and pity of these things.

       *   *   *

The second whip was Kitty Myngs,
Still but a lad but keen and quick
(Son of old Myngs, who farmed the Wick),
A horse-mouthed lad who knew his work.
He rode the big black horse, the Turk.

And longed to be a huntsman bold.
He had the horse-look, sharp and old,
With much good-nature in his face.
His passion was to go the pace,
His blood was crying for a taming.
He was the Devil's chick for gaming,
He was a rare good lad to box.
He sometimes had a main of cocks
Down at the Flags. His job with hounds
At present kept his blood in bounds
From rioting and running hare.
Tom Dansey made him have a care.
He worshipped Dansey heart and soul.
To be a huntsman was his goal;
To be with hounds, to charge full tilt
Blackthorns that made the gentry wilt
Was his ambition and his hope.
He was a hot colt needing rope,
He was too quick to speak his passion
To suit his present huntsman's fashion.

*   *   *

The huntsman, Robin Dawe, looked round,
He sometimes called a favourite hound,
Gently, to see the creature turn,
Look happy up and wag his stern.
He smiled and nodded and saluted
To those who hailed him, as it suited.
And patted Pip's, his hunter's neck.
His new pink was without a speck.
He was a red-faced smiling fellow,
His voice clear tenor, full and mellow,
His eyes, all fire, were black and small.
He had been smashed in many a fall.

His eyebrow had a white curved mark
Left by the bright shoe of The Lark
Down in a ditch by Seven Springs.
His coat had all been trod to strings,
His ribs laid bare and shoulder broken,
Being jumped on down at Water's Oaken
The time his horse came down and rolled.
His face was of the country mould
Such as the mason sometimes cutted
On English moulding-ends which jutted
Out of the church walls, centuries since.
And as you never know the quince,
How good he is, until you try,
So, in Dawe's face, what met the eye
Was only part; what lay behind
Was English character and mind,
Great kindness, delicate sweet feeling
(Most shy, most clever in concealing
Its depth) for beauty of all sorts,
Great manliness and love of sports,
A grave, wise thoughtfulness and truth,
A merry fun outlasting youth,
A courage terrible to see,
And mercy for his enemy.

He had a clean-shaved face, but kept
A hedge of whisker neatly clipped,
A narrow strip or picture-frame
(Old Dawe, the woodman, did the same),
Under his chin from ear to ear.

        *   *   *

But now the resting hounds gave cheer,

Joyful and Arrogant and Catch-him
Smelt the glad news and ran to snatch him:
The Master's dogcart turned the bend.
Damsel and Skylark knew their friend,
A thrill ran through the pack like fire
And little whimpers ran in quire.
The horses cocked and pawed and whickered
Young Cothill's chaser kicked and bickered
And stood on end and struck out sparks,
Joyful and Catch-him sang like larks.
There was the Master in the trap,
Clutching old Roman in his lap,
Old Roman, crazy for his brothers,
And putting frenzy in the others
To set them at the dogcart wheels,
With thrusting heads and little squeals.

*　　*　　*

The Master put old Roman by,
And eyed the thrusters heedfully.
He called a few pet hounds and fed
Three special friends with scraps of bread,
Then peeled his wraps, climbed down and strode
Through all those clamourers in the road,
Saluted friends, looked round the crowd,
Saw Harridew's three girls and bowed,
Then took White Rabbit from the groom.

*　　*　　*

He was Sir Peter Bynd, of Coombe;
Past sixty now, though hearty still,
A living picture of good-will,
An old, grave soldier, sweet and kind,
A courtier with a knightly mind,

Who felt whatever thing he thought.
His face was scarred, for he had fought
Five wars for us. Within his face
Courage and power had their place,
Rough energy, decision, force.
He smiled about him from his horse.
He had a welcome and salute
For all, on horse or wheel or foot
Whatever kind of life each followed.
His tanned, drawn cheeks looked old and hollowed,
But still his bright blue eyes were young,
And when the pack crashed into tongue,
And stanch White Rabbit shook like fire,
He sent him at it like a flier,
And lived with hounds while horses could.

*   *   *

'They'm lying in the Ghost Heath Wood,
Sir Peter,' said an earth-stopper
(Old Baldy Hill), 'you'll find 'em there.
'Z I come'd across I smell 'em plain.
There's one up back, down Tuttock's drain,
But, Lord, it's just a bog, the Tuttocks,
Hounds would be swallered to the buttocks.
Heath Wood, Sir Peter's best to draw.'

*   *   *

Sir Peter gave two minutes' law
For Kingston Challow and his daughter;
He said, 'They're late. We'll start the slaughter.
Ghost Heath, then, Dansey. We'll be going.'

*   *   *

Now, at his word, the tide was flowing.
Off went Maroon, off went the hounds,

Down road, then off, to Chols Elm Grounds,
Across soft turf with dead leaves cleaving
And hillocks that the mole was heaving,
Mild going to those trotting feet.
After the scarlet coats the meet
Came clopping up the grass in spate;
They poached the trickle at the gate
Their horses' feet sucked at the mud,
Excitement in the horses' blood.
Cocked forward every ear and eye,
They quivered as the hounds went by,
They trembled when they first trod grass,
They would not let another pass,
They scattered wide up Chols Elm Hill.

The wind was westerly but still,
The sky a high fair-weather cloud,
Like meadows ridge-and-furrow ploughed,
Just glinting sun but scarcely moving.
Blackbirds and thrushes thought of loving,
Catkins were out; the day seemed tense
It was so still. At every fence
Cow-parsley pushed its thin green fern.
White-violet leaves showed at the burn.

★   ★   ★

Young Cothill let his chaser go
Round Chols Elm Field a turn or so
To soothe his edge. The riders went
Chatting and laughing and content
In groups of two or three together,
The hounds, a flock of shaking feather,
Bobbed on ahead, past Chols Elm Cop,
The horses' shoes went clip-a-clop,

Along the stony cart-track there,
The little spinney was all bare,
But in the earth-moist winter day
The scarlet coats twixt tree and spray
The glistening horses pressing on,
The brown-faced lads, Bill, Dick and John,
And all the hurry to arrive,
Were beautiful like spring alive.

     *   *   *

The hounds melted away with Master,
The tanned lads ran, the field rode faster,
The chatter joggled in the throats
Of riders bumping by like boats,
'We really ought to hunt a bye day'
'Fine day for scent,' 'A fly or die day.'
'They chopped a bagman in the check,
He had a collar round his neck.'
'Old Ridden's girl's a pretty flapper.'
'That Vaughan's a cad, the whippersnapper.'
'I tell 'ee, lads, I seed 'em plain
Down in the Rough at Shifford's Main,
Old Squire stamping like a Duke,
So red with blood I thought he'd puke
In appleplexie, as they do.
Miss Jane stood just as white as dew
And heard him out in just white heat,
And then she trimmed him down a treat.
About Miss Lou it was, or Carrie
(She'd be a pretty peach to marry).'

     *   *   *

'Her'll draw up-wind, so us'll go
Down by the furze, we'll see 'em so.'

     *   *   *

'Look, there they go, lad!'

There they went
Across the brook and up the bent,
Past Primrose Wood, past Brady Ride,
Along Ghost Heath to cover side.
The bobbing scarlet, trotting pack,
Turf scatters tossed behind each back,
Some horses blowing with a whinny,
A jam of horses in the spinney,
Close to the ride-gate; leather straining.
Saddles all creaking, men complaining,
Chaffing each other as they past,
On Ghost Heath turf they trotted fast.

    ★ ★ ★

Now as they neared the Ghost Heath Wood
Some riders grumbled, 'What's the good?
It's shot all day and poached all night.
We shall draw blank and lose the light,
And lose the scent and lose the day.
Why can't he draw Hope Goneaway,
Or Tuttocks Wood, instead of this?
There's no fox here, there never is.'

    ★ ★ ★

But as he trotted up to cover
Robin was watching to discover
What chance there was, and many a token
Told him that though no hound had spoken,
Most of them stirred to something there.
The old hounds' muzzles searched the air,
Thin ghosts of scents were in their teeth
From foxes which had crossed the Heath

Not very many hours before.
'We'll find,' he said, 'I'll bet, a score.'

    ★   ★   ★

Along Ghost Heath they trotted well,
The hoof-cuts made the bruised earth smell,
The shaken brambles scattered drops,
Stray pheasants kukkered out of copse,
Cracking the twigs down with their knockings
And planing out of sight with cockings;
A scut or two lopped white to bramble.

    ★   ★   ★

And now they gathered to the gamble
At Ghost Heath Wood on Ghost Heath Down,
The hounds went crackling through the brown
Dry stalks of bracken killed by frost.
The wood stood silent in its host
Of halted trees all winter bare.
The boughs, like veins that suck the air,
Stretched tense, the last leaf scarcely stirred,
There came no song from any bird;
The darkness of the wood stood still
Waiting for fate on Ghost Heath Hill.

    ★   ★   ★

The whips crept to the sides to view,
The Master gave the nod, and 'Leu,
Leu in. Ed-hoick, ed-hoick. Leu in!'
Went Robin, cracking through the whin
And through the hedge-gap into cover.
The binders crashed as hounds went over,
And cock-cock-cock the pheasants rose.
Then up went stern and down went nose,
And Robin's cheerful tenor cried,

Through hazel-scrub and stub and ride:
'Oh, wind him! beauties, push him out,
Yooi, on to him, Yahout, Yahout,
Oh, push him out, Yooi, wind him, wind him!'
The beauties burst the scrub to find him;
They nosed the warren's clipped green lawn,
The bramble and the broom were drawn,
The covert's northern end was blank.
They turned to draw along the bank
Through thicker cover than the Rough,
Through three-and-four-year understuff
Where Robin's forearm screened his eyes;
'Yooi, find him, beauties,' came his cries.
'Hark, hark to Daffodil,' the laughter
Fal'n from his horn, brought whimpers after,
For ends of scents were everywhere.
He said, 'This Hope's a likely lair,
And there's his billets, grey and furred.
And George, he's moving, there's a bird.'

*   *   *

A blue uneasy jay was chacking
(A swearing screech, like tearing sacking)
From tree to tree, as in pursuit,
He said, 'That's it. There's fox afoot.
And there, they're feathering, there she speaks.
Good Daffodil, good Tarrybreeks,
Hark there on Daffodil, hark, hark!'
The mild horn's note, the soft-flaked spark
Of music fell on that rank scent.
From heart to wild heart magic went.

The whimpering quivered, quavered, rose.
'Daffodil has it. There she goes.

Oh, hark to her!' With wild high crying
From frantic hearts the hounds went flying
To Daffodil, for that rank taint.
A waft of it came warm but faint
In Robin's mouth, and faded so.
'First find a fox, then let him go,'
Cried Robin Dawe. 'For any sake
Ring, Charley, till you're fit to break.'
He cheered his beauties like a lover
And charged beside them into cover.

PART II

ON old Cold Crendon's windy tops
Grows wintrily Blown Hilcote Copse,
Wind-bitten beech with badger barrows,
Where brocks eat wasp-grubs with their marrows
And foxes lie on short-grassed turf,
Nose between paws, to hear the surf
Of wind in the beeches drowsily.
There was our fox bred lustily
Three years before, and there he berthed,
Under the beech-roots snugly earthed,
With a roof of flint and a floor of chalk
And ten bitten hens' heads each on its stalk,
Some rabbits' paws, some fur from scuts,
A badger's corpse and a smell of guts.
And there on the night before my tale
He trotted out for a point in the vale.

*   *   *

He saw, from the cover edge, the valley
Go trooping down with its droops of sally
To the brimming river's lipping bend,
And a light in the inn at Water's End.
He heard the owl go hunting by
And the shriek of the mouse the owl made die,
And the purr of the owl as he tore the red
Strings from between his claws and fed;
The smack of joy of the horny lips
Marbled green with the blobby strips.
He saw the farms where the dogs were barking,
Cold Crendon Court and Copsecote Larking;
The fault with the spring as bright as gleed,
Green-slash-laced with water-weed.
A glare in the sky still marked the town,
Though all folk slept and the blinds were down,
The street lamps watched the empty square,
The night-cat sang his evil there.

*   *   *

The fox's nose tipped up and round,
Since smell is a part of sight and sound.
Delicate smells were drifting by,
The sharp nose flaired them heedfully;
Patridges in the clover stubble,
Crouched in a ring for the stoat to nubble.
Rabbit bucks beginning to box;
A scratching place for the pheasant cocks,
A hare in the dead grass near the drain,
And another smell like the spring again.

*   *   *

A faint rank taint like April coming,
It cocked his ears and his blood went drumming,
D.—9

For somewhere out by Ghost Heath Stubs
Was a roving vixen wanting cubs.
Over the valley, floating faint
On a warmth of windflaw, came the taint;
He cocked his ears, he upped his brush,
And he went upwind like an April thrush.

*   *   *

By the Roman Road to Braiches Ridge,
Where the fallen willow makes a bridge.
Over the brook by White Hart's Thorn
To the acres thin with pricking corn,
Over the sparse green hair of the wheat,
By the Clench Brook Mill at Clench Brook Leat,
Through Cowfoot Pastures to Nonely Stevens,
And away to Poltrewood St Jevons.
Past Tott Hill Down all snaked with meuses,
Past Clench St Michael and Naunton Crucis,
Past Howle's Oak Farm where the raving brain
Of a dog who heard him foamed his chain;
Then off, as the farmer's window opened,
Past Stonepits Farm to Upton Hope End,
Over short sweet grass and worn flint arrows
And the three dumb hows of Tencombe Barrows.
And away and away with a rolling scramble,
Through the sally and up the bramble,
With a nose for the smells the night wind carried,
And his red fell clean for being married;
For clicketting time and Ghost Heath Wood
Had put the violet in his blood.

*   *   *

At Tencombe Rings near the Manor Linney
His foot made the great black stallion whinny,
And the stallion's whinny aroused the stable

And the bloodhound bitches stretched their cable,
And the clink of the bloodhounds' chain aroused
The sweet-breathed kye as they chewed and drowsed,
And the stir of the cattle changed the dream
Of the cat in the loft to tense green gleam.
The red-wattled black cock hot from Spain
Crowed from his perch for dawn again,
His breast-pufft hens, one-legged on perch,
Gurgled, beak-down, like men in church,
They crooned in the dark, lifting one red eye
In the raftered roost as the fox went by.

      ★   ★   ★

By Tencombe Regis and Slaughters Court,
Through the great grass square of Roman Fort,
By Nun's Wood Yews and the Hungry Hill,
And the Corpse Way Stones all standing still.
By Seven Springs Mead to Deerlip Brook,
And a lolloping leap to Water Hook.
Then with eyes like sparks and his blood awoken,
Over the grass to Water's Oaken,
And over the hedge and into ride
In Ghost Heath Wood for his roving bride.

      ★   ★   ★

Before the dawn he had loved and fed
And found a kennel, and gone to bed
On a shelf of grass in a thick of gorse
That would bleed a hound and blind a horse.
There he slept in the mild west weather
With his nose and brush well tucked together,
He slept like a child, who sleeps yet hears
With the self who needs neither eyes nor ears.

      ★   ★   ★

He slept while the pheasant cock untucked
His head from his wing flew down and kukked,
While the drove of the starlings whirred and wheeled
Out of the ash-trees into field,
While with great black flags that flogged and paddled
The rooks went out to the plough and straddled,
Straddled wide on the moist red cheese
Of the furrows driven at Uppat's Leas.

*   *   *

Down in the village men awoke,
The chimneys breathed with a faint blue smoke.
The fox slept on, though tweaks and twitches,
Due to his dreams, ran down his flitches.

*   *   *

The cows were milked and the yards were sluiced,
And the cocks and hens let out of roost,
Windows were opened, mats were beaten,
All men's breakfasts were cooked and eaten;
But out in the gorse on the grassy shelf
The sleeping fox looked after himself.

*   *   *

Deep in his dream he heard the life
Of the woodland seek for food or wife,
The hop of a stoat, a buck that thumped,
The squeal of a rat as a weasel jumped,
The blackbird's chackering scattering crying,
The rustling bents from the rabbits flying,
Cows in a byre, and distant men,
And Condicote church-clock striking ten.

*   *   *

At eleven o'clock a boy went past,
With a rough-haired terrier following fast.

The boy's sweet whistle and dog's quick yap
Woke the fox from out of his nap.

      *   *   *

He rose and stretched till the claws in his pads
Stuck hornily out like long black gads.
He listened a while, and his nose went round
To catch the smell of the distant sound.

      *   *   *

The windward smells came free from taint—
They were rabbit, strongly, with lime-kiln, faint,
A wild-duck, likely, at Sars Holt Pond,
And sheep on the Sars Holt Down beyond.

      *   *   *

The leeward smells were much less certain,
For the Ghost Heath Hill was like a curtain,
Yet vague, from the leeward, now and then,
Came muffled sounds like the sound of men.

      *   *   *

He moved to his right to a clearer space,
And all his soul came into his face,
Into his eyes and into his nose,
As over the hill a murmur rose.
His ears were cocked and his keen nose flaired,
He sneered with his lips till his teeth were bared,
He trotted right and lifted a pad
Trying to test what foes he had.

      *   *   *

On Ghost Heath turf was a steady drumming
Which sounded like horses quickly coming,
It died as the hunt went down the dip,
Then Malapert yelped at Myng's whip.
A bright iron horseshoe clinked on stone,
Then a man's voice spoke, not one alone,

Then a burst of laughter, swiftly still,
Muffled away by Ghost Heath Hill.
Then, indistinctly, the clop, clip, clep,
On Brady Ride, of a horse's step.
Then silence, then, in a burst, much clearer,
Voices and horses coming nearer,
And another noise, of a pit-pat beat
On the Ghost Hill grass, of foxhound feet.

   ★   ★   ★

He sat on his haunches listening hard,
While his mind went over the compass card.
Men were coming and rest was done,
But he still had time to get fit to run;
He could outlast horse and outrace hound,
But men were devils from Lobs's Pound.
Scent was burning, the going good,
The world one lust for a fox's blood,
The main earths stopped and the drains put to,
And fifteen miles to the land he knew.
But of all the ills, the ill least pleasant
Was to run in the light when men were present.
Men in the fields to shout and sign
For a lift of hounds to a fox's line.
Men at the earth, at the long point's end,
Men at each check and none his friend,
Guessing each shift that a fox contrives;
But still, needs must when the devil drives.

   ★   ★   ★

He readied himself, then a soft horn blew,
Then a clear voice carolled, 'Ed-hoick! Eleu!'
Then the wood-end rang with the clear voice crying
And the cackle of scrub where hounds were trying.

Then the horn blew nearer, a hound's voice quivered,
Then another, then more, till his body shivered,
He left his kennel and trotted thence
With his ears flexed back and his nerves all tense.

He trotted down with his nose intent
For a fox's line to cross his scent,
It was only fair (he being a stranger)
That the native fox should have the danger.
Danger was coming, so swift, so swift,
That the pace of his trot began to lift
The blue-winged Judas, a jay began
Swearing, hounds whimpered, air stank of man.

                  *   *   *

He hurried his trotting, he now felt frighted,
It was his poor body made hounds excited.
He felt as he ringed the great wood through
That he ought to make for the land he knew.

                  *   *   *

Then the hounds' excitement quivered and quickened,
Then a horn blew death till his marrow sickened,
Then the wood behind was a crash of cry
For the blood in his veins; it made him fly.

                  *   *   *

They were on his line; it was death to stay.
He must make for home by the shortest way,
But with all this yelling and all this wrath
And all these devils, how find a path?

                  *   *   *

He ran like a stag to the wood's north corner,
Where the hedge was thick and the ditch a yawner,
But the scarlet glimpse of Myngs on Turk,
Watching the woodside, made him shirk.

He ringed the wood and looked at the south.
What wind there was blew into his mouth.
But close to the woodland's blackthorn thicket
Was Dansey, still as a stone, on picket.
At Dansey's back were a twenty more
Watching the cover and pressing fore.

*   *   *

The fox drew in and flaired with his muzzle.
Death was there if he messed the puzzle.
There were men without and hounds within,
A crying that stiffened the hair on skin.
Teeth in cover and death without,
Both deaths coming, and no way out.

*   *   *

His nose ranged swiftly, his heart beat fast,
Then a crashing cry rose up in a blast,
Then horse-hooves trampled, then horses' flitches
Burst their way through the hazel switches.
Then the horn again made the hounds like mad,
And a man, quite near, said, 'Found, by Gad!'
And a man, quite near, said, 'Now he'll break.
Larks Leybourne Copse is the line he'll take.'
And men moved up with their talk and stink
And the traplike noise of the horseshoe clink.
Men whose coming meant death from teeth
In a worrying wrench, with him beneath.

*   *   *

The fox sneaked down by the cover side
(With his ears flexed back) as a snake would glide;
He took the ditch at the cover-end,
He hugged the ditch as his only friend.
The blackbird cock with the golden beak
Got out of his way with a jabbering shriek,

And the shriek told Tom on the raking bay
That for eighteenpence he was gone away.

*   *   *

He ran in the hedge in the triple growth
Of bramble and hawthorn, glad of both,
Till a couple of fields were past, and then
Came the living death of the dread of men.

*   *   *

Then, as he listened, he heard a 'Hoy!'
Tom Dansey's horn and 'Awa-wa-woy!'
Then all hounds crying with all their forces,
Then a thundering down of seventy horses.
Robin Dawe's horn and halloes of 'Hey
Hark Hollar, Hoik!' and 'Gone away!'
'Hark Hollar Hoik!' and a smack of the whip,
A yelp as a tail hound caught the clip.
'Hark Hollar, Hark Hollar!' then Robin made
Pip go crash through the cut and laid.
Hounds were over and on his line
With a head like bees upon Tipple Tine.
The sound of the nearness sent a flood
Of terror of death through the fox's blood.
He upped his brush and he cocked his nose,
And he went upwind as a racer goes.

*   *   *

Bold Robin Dawe was over first,
Cheering his hounds on at the burst;
The field were spurring to be in it.
'Hold hard, sirs, give them half a minute,'
Came from Sir Peter on his white.
The hounds went romping with delight
Over the grass and got together,
The tail hounds galloped hell-for-leather

After the pack at Myngs's yell.
A cry like every kind of bell
Rang from these rompers as they raced.

*   *   *

The riders, thrusting to be placed,
Jammed down their hats and shook their horses;
The hounds romped past with all their forces,
They crashed into the blackthorn fence.
The scent was heavy on their sense,
So hot, it seemed the living thing,
It made the blood within them sing;
Gusts of it made their hackles rise,
Hot gulps of it were agonies
Of joy, and thirst for blood and passion.
'Forward!' cried Robin, 'that's the fashion.'
He raced beside his pack to cheer.

The field's noise died upon his ear,
A faint horn, far behind, blew thin
In cover, lest some hound were in.
Then instantly the great grass rise
Shut field and cover from his eyes,
He and his racers were alone.
'A dead fox or a broken bone,'
Said Robin, peering for his prey.

*   *   *

The rise, which shut the field away,
Showed him the vale's great map spread out,
The down's lean flank and thrusting snout,
Pale pastures, red-brown plough, dark wood,
Blue distance, still as solitude,
Glitter of water here and there,

The trees so delicately bare,
The dark green gorse and bright green holly.
'O glorious God,' he said, 'how jolly!'
And there downhill two fields ahead
The lolloping red dog-fox sped
Over Poor Pastures to the brook.
He grasped these things in one swift look,
Then dived into the bullfinch heart
Through thorns that ripped his sleeves apart
And skutched new blood upon his brow.
'His point's Lark's Leybourne Covers now,'
Said Robin, landing with a grunt.
'Forrard, my beautifuls!'

                                The hunt
Followed downhill to race with him,
White Rabbit, with his swallow's skim,
Drew within hail. 'Quick burst, Sir Peter.'
'A traveller. Nothing could be neater.
Making for Godsdown Clumps, I take it?'
'Lark's Leybourne, sir, if he can make it.
Forrard!'

                Bill Ridden thundered down,
His big mouth grinned beneath his frown,
The hounds were going away from horses.
He saw the glint of watercourses,
Yell Brook and Wittold's Dyke, ahead,
His horseshoes sliced the green turf red.
Young Cothill's chaser rushed and past him,
Nob Manor, running next, said 'Blast him!
The poet chap who thinks he rides,'
Hugh Colway's mare made straking strides

Across the grass, the Colonel next,
Then Squire, volleying oaths, and vext,
Fighting his hunter for refusing;
Bell Ridden, like a cutter cruising,
Sailing the grass; then Cob on Warder,
Then Minton Price upon Marauder;
Ock Gurney with his eyes intense,
Burning as with a different sense,
His big mouth muttering glad 'By damns!'
Then Pete, crouched down from head to hams,
Rapt like a saint, bright focussed flame;
Bennett, with devils in his wame,
Chewing black cud and spitting slanting;
Copse scattering jests and Stukely ranting;
Sal Ridden taking line from Dansey;
Long Robert forcing Necromancy;
A dozen more with bad beginnings;
Myngs riding hard to snatch an innings.
A wild last hound with high shrill yelps
Smacked forrard with some whipthong skelps.
Then last of all, at top of rise,
The crowd on foot, all gasps and eyes;
The run up hill had winded them.

*   *   *

They saw the Yell Brook like a gem
Blue in the grass a short mile on;
They heard faint cries, but hounds were gone
A good eight fields and out of sight,
Except a rippled glimmer white
Going away with dying cheering,
And scarlet flappings disappearing,
And scattering horses going, going,

Going like mad, White Rabbit snowing
Far on ahead, a loose horse taking
Fence after fence with stirrups shaking,
And scarlet specks and dark specks dwindling.

    *   *   *

Nearer, were twigs knocked into kindling,
A much bashed fence still dropping stick,
Flung clods still quivering from the kick;
Cut hoof-marks pale in cheesy clay,
The horse-smell blowing clean away;
Birds flitting back into the cover.
One last faint cry, then all was over.
The hunt had been, and found, and gone,

    *   *   *

At Neaking's Farm three furlongs on,
Hounds raced across the Waysmore Road,
Where many of the riders slowed
To tittup down a grassy lane
Which led as hounds led in the main,
And gave no danger of a fall.
There as they tittupped one and all,
Big Twenty Stone came scattering by,
His great mare made the hoof-casts fly.
'By leave!' he cried. 'Come on! Come up!
This fox is running like a tup;
Let's leave this lane and get to terms,
No sense in crawling here like worms.
Come, let me pass and let me start.
This fox is running like a hart,
And this is going to be a run.
Come on, I want to see the fun.
Thanky. By leave! Now, Maiden, do it.'
He faced the fence and put her through it,

Shielding his eyes lest spikes should blind him;
The crashing blackthorn closed behind him.
Mud-scatters chased him as he scudded;
His mare's ears cocked, her neat feet thudded.

       ★   ★   ★

The kestrel cruising over meadow
Watched the hunt gallop on his shadow,
Wee figures, almost at a stand,
Crossing the multicoloured land,
Slow as a shadow on a dial.

       ★   ★   ★

Some horses, swerving at a trial,
Balked at a fence: at gates they bunched.
The mud about the gates was dunched
Like German cheese; men pushed for places
And kicked the mud into the faces
Of those who made them room to pass.
The half-mile's gallop on the grass
Had tailed them out and warmed their blood.
'His point's the Banner Barton Wood.'
'That, or Goat's Gorse.' 'A stinger, this.'
'You're right in that; by Jove, it is.'
'An upwind travelling fox, by George!'
'They say Tom viewed him at the forge.'
'Well, let me pass and let's be on.'

       ★   ★   ★

They crossed the lane to Tolderton,
The hill-marl died to valley clay,
And there before them ran the grey
Yell Water, swirling as it ran,
The Yell Brook of the hunting man.
The hunters eyed it and were grim.

       ★   ★   ★

They saw the water snaking slim
Ahead, like silver; they could see
(Each man) his pollard willow-tree
Firming the bank; they felt their horses
Catch the gleam's hint and gather forces;
They heard the men behind draw near.
Each horse was trembling as a spear
Trembles in hand when tense to hurl.
They saw the brimmed brook's eddies curl;
The willow-roots like water-snakes;
The beaten holes the ratten makes.
They heard the water's rush; they heard
Hugh Colway's mare come like a bird;
A faint cry from the hounds ahead,
Then saddle-strain, the bright hooves' tread,
Quick words, the splash of mud, the launch,
The sick hope that the bank be staunch,
Then Souse, with Souse to left and right.
Maroon across, Sir Peter's white
Down but pulled up, Tom over, Hugh
Mud to the hat but over too,
Well splashed by Squire, who was in.

*   *   *

With draggled pink stuck close to skin
The Squire leaned from bank and hauled
His mired horse's rein; he bawled
For help from each man racing by.
'What, help you pull him out? Not I.
What made you pull him in?' They said.
Nob Manor cleared and turned his head,
And cried, 'Wade up. The ford's upstream.'
Ock Gurney in a cloud of steam

Stood by his dripping cob and wrung
The taste of brook mud from his tongue,
And scraped his poor cob's pasterns clean.
'Lord, what a crowner we've a-been.
This jumping brook's a mucky job.'
He muttered, grinning, 'Lord, poor cob!
Now, sir, let me.' He turned to Squire
And cleared his hunter from the mire
By skill and sense and strength of arm.

*   *   *

Meanwhile the fox passed Nonesuch Farm,
Keeping the spinney on his right.
Hounds raced him here with all their might
Along the short firm grass, like fire.
The cowman viewed him from the byre
Lolloping on, six fields ahead,
Then hounds, still carrying such a head
It made him stare, then Rob on Pip,
Sailing the great grass like a ship,
Then grand Maroon in all his glory,
Sweeping his strides, his great chest hoary
With foam fleck and the pale hill-marl.
They strode the Leet, they flew the Snarl,
They knocked the nuts at Nonesuch Mill,
Raced up the spur of Gallows Hill
And viewed him there. The line he took
Was Tineton and the Pantry Brook,
Going like fun and hounds like mad.
Tom glanced to see what friends he had
Still within sight, before he turned
The ridge's shoulder; he discerned,
One field away, young Cothill sailing

Easily up. Pete Gurney failing,
Hugh Colway quartering on Sir Peter,
Bill waiting on the mare to beat her,
Sal Ridden skirting to the right.
A horse, with stirrups flashing bright
Over his head at every stride,
Looked like the Major's; Tom espied
Far back a scarlet speck of man
Running, and straddling as he ran.
Charles Copse was up, Nob Manor followed,
Then Bennett's big-boned black that wallowed,
Clumsy, but with the strength of ten.
Then black and brown and scarlet men,
Brown horses, white and black and grey,
Scattered a dozen fields away.
The shoulder shut the scene away.

★   ★   ★

From the Gallows Hill to the Tineton Copse
There were ten ploughed fields, like ten full-stops,
All wet red clay, where a horse's foot
Would be swathed, feet thick, like an ash-tree root.
The fox raced on, on the headlands firm,
Where his swift feet scared the coupling worm;
The rooks rose raving to curse him raw,
He snarled a sneer at their swoop and caw.
Then on, then on, down a half-ploughed field
Where a ship-like plough drove glitter-keeled,
With a bay horse near and a white horse leading,
And a man saying 'Zook', and the red earth bleeding.
He gasped as he saw the ploughman drop
The stilts and swear at the team to stop.
The ploughman ran in his red clay clogs,
Crying, 'Zick un, Towzer; zick, good dogs!'

D.—10

A couple of wire-haired lurchers lean
Arose from his wallet, nosing keen;
With a rushing swoop they were on his track,
Putting chest to stubble to bite his back.
He swerved from his line with the curs at heel,
The teeth as they missed him clicked like steel.
With a worrying snarl, they quartered on him,
While the ploughman shouted, 'Zick; upon him.'

*   *   *

The lurcher dogs soon shot their bolt,
And the fox raced on by the Hazel Holt,
Down the dead grass tilt to the sandstone gash
Of the Pantry Brook at Tineton Ash.
The loitering water, flooded full,
Had yeast on its lip like raddled wool,
It was wrinkled over with Arab script
Of eddies that twisted up and slipped
The stepping-stones had a rush about them,
So the fox plunged in and swam without them.

*   *   *

He crossed to the cattle's drinking shallow,
Firmed up with rush and the roots of mallow;
He wrung his coat from his draggled bones
And romped away from the Sarsen Stones.

*   *   *

A sneaking glance with his ears flexed back
Made sure that his scent had failed the pack.
For the red clay, good for corn and roses,
Was cold for scent and brought hounds to noses

*   *   *

He slackened pace by the Tineton Tree
(A vast hollow ash-tree grown in three),

He wriggled a shake and padded slow,
Not sure if the hounds were on or no.

★   ★   ★

A horn blew faint, then he heard the sounds
Of a cantering huntsman, lifting hounds;
The ploughman had raised his hat for sign,
And the hounds were lifted and on his line.
He heard the splash in the Pantry Brook,
And a man's voice: 'Thiccy's the line he took.'
And a clear 'Yoi doit!' and a whimpering quaver,
Though the lurcher dogs had dulled the savour.

★   ★   ★

The fox went off while the hounds made halt,
And the horses breathed and the field found fault,
But the whimpering rose to a crying crash
By the hollow ruin of Tineton Ash.
Then again the kettledrum horsehooves beat,
And the green blades bent to the fox's feet,
And the cry rose keen not far behind
Of the 'Blood, blood, blood,' in the foxhounds' mind.

★   ★   ★

The fox was strong, he was full of running,
He could run for an hour and then be cunning,
But the cry behind him made him chill,
They were nearer now and they meant to kill.
They meant to run him until his blood
Clogged on his heart as his brush with mud,
Till his back bent up and his tongue hung flagging,
And his belly and brush were filthed from dragging.
Till he crouched stone-still, dead-beat and dirty,
With nothing but teeth against the thirty.
And all the way to that blinding end
He would meet with men and have none his friends:

Men to holloa and men to run him,
With stones to stagger and yells to stun him;
Men to head him, with whips to beat him,
Teeth to mangle and mouths to eat him.
And all the way, that wild high crying.
To cold his blood with the thought of dying,
The horn and the cheer, and the drum-like thunder
Of the horsehooves stamping the meadows under.
He upped his brush and went with a will
For the Sarsen Stones on Wan Dyke Hill.

*   *   *

As he ran the meadow by Tineton Church
A christening party left the porch;
They stood stock still as he pounded by,
They wished him luck but they thought he'd die.
The toothless babe in his long white coat
Looked delicate meat, the fox took note;
But the sight of them grinning there, pointing finger,
Made him put on steam till he went a stinger.

*   *   *

Past Tineton Church, over Tineton Waste,
With the lolloping ease of a fox's haste,
The fur on his chest blown dry with the air,
His brush still up and his cheek-teeth bare.
Over the Waste, where the ganders grazed,
The long swift lilt of his loping lazed,
His ears cocked up as his blood ran higher,
He saw his point, and his eyes took fire.
The Wan Dyke Hill with its fir-tree barren,
Its dark of gorse and its rabbit-warren,
The Dyke on its heave like a tightened girth,
And holes in the Dyke where a fox might earth.

He had rabbited there long months before,
The earths were deep and his need was sore;
The way was new, but he took a bearing,
And rushed like a blown ship billow-sharing.

*   *   *

Off Tineton Common to Tineton Dean,
Where the wind-hid elders pushed with green;
Through the Dean's thin cover across the lane,
And up Midwinter to King of Spain.
Old Joe, at digging his garden grounds,
Said: 'A fox, being hunted; where be hounds?
O lord, my back, to be young again,
'Stead a zellin' zider in King of Spain!
O hark! I hear 'em, O sweet, O sweet.
Why there be redcoat in Gearge's wheat.
And there be redcoat, and there they gallop.
Thur go a browncoat down a wallop.
Quick, Ellen, quick! Come, Susan, fly!
Here'm hounds. I zeed the fox go by,
Go by like thunder, go by like blasting,
With his girt white teeth all looking ghasting.
Look, there come hounds! Hark, hear 'em crying?
Lord, belly to stubble, ain't they flying!
There's huntsman, there. The fox come past
(As I was digging) as fast as fast.
He's only been gone a minute by;
A girt dark dog as pert as pye.'

Ellen and Susan came out scattering
Brooms and dustpans till all was clattering;
They saw the pack come head-to-foot
Running like racers, nearly mute;

Robin and Dansey quartering near
All going gallop like startled deer.
A half-dozen flitting scarlets showing
In the thin green Dean where the pines were growing.
Black coats and brown coats thrusting and spurring,
Sending the partridge coveys whirring.
Then a rattle uphill and a clop up lane,
It emptied the bar of the King of Spain.

   ★   ★   ★

Tom left his cider, Dick left his bitter,
Granfer James left his pipe and spitter;
Out they came from the sawdust floor.
They said, 'They'm going.' They said, 'O Lor'!'

The fox raced on, up the Barton Balks,
With a crackle of kex on the nettle stalks,
Over Hammond's grass to the dark green line
Of the larch-wood smelling of turpentine.
Scratch Steven Larches, black to the sky,
A sadness breathing with one long sigh,
Grey ghosts of trees under funeral plumes,
A mist of twig over soft brown glooms.
As he entered the wood he heard the smacks,
Chip-jar, of the fir-pole feller's axe.
He swerved to the left to a broad green ride,
Where a boy made him rush for the farther side.
He swerved to the left, to the Barton Road,
But there were the timberers come to load—
Two timber-carts and a couple of carters
With straps round their knees instead of garters.
He swerved to the right, straight down the wood,
The carters watched him, the boy hallooed.

He leaped from the larch-wood into tillage,
The cobbler's garden of Barton village.

       ★   ★   ★

The cobbler bent at his wooden foot,
Beating sprigs in a broken boot;
He wore old glasses with thick horn rim,
He scowled at his work, for his sight was dim.
His face was dingy, his lips were grey,
From primming sparrowbills day by day.
As he turned his boot he heard a noise
At his garden-end, and he thought, 'It's boys.'

       ★   ★   ★

He saw his cat nip up on the shed,
Where her back arched up till it touched her head;
He saw his rabbit race round and round
Its little black box three feet from ground.
His six hens cluckered and flocked to perch,
'That's boys,' said cobbler, 'so I'll go search.'
He reached his stick and blinked in his wrath,
When he saw a fox in his garden path.

       ★   ★   ★

The fox swerved left and scrambled out,
Knocking crinked green shells from the brussels-sprout
He scrambled out through the cobbler's paling,
And up Pill's orchard to Purton's Tailing,
Across the plough at the top of bent,
Through the heaped manure to kill his scent,
Over to Aldam's, up to Cappell's,
Past Nursery Lot with its whitewashed apples,
Past Colston's Broom, past Gaunt's, past Shere's,
Past Foxwhelps' Oasts with their hooded ears,
Past Monk's Ash Clerewell, past Beggars' Oak,
Past the great elms blue with the Hinton smoke.

Along Long Hinton to Hinton Green,
Where the wind-washed steeple stood serene
With its golden bird still sailing air.
Past Banner Barton, past Chipping Bare,
Past Maddings Hollow, down Dundry Dip,
And up Goose Grass to the Sailing Ship.

★   ★   ★

The three black firs of the Ship stood still
On the bare chalk heave of the Dundry Hill.
The fox looked back as he slackened past
The scaled red-bole of the mizen-mast.

★   ★   ★

There they were coming, mute but swift—
A scarlet smear in the blackthorn rift,
A white horse rising, a dark horse flying,
And the hungry hounds too tense for crying.
Stormcock leading, his stern spear straight,
Racing as though for a piece of plate,
Little speck horsemen field on field;
Then Dansey viewed him and Robin squealed.

★   ★   ★

At the 'View Halloo!' the hounds went frantic,
Back went Stormcock and up went Antic,
Up went Skylark as Antic sped,
It was zest to blood how they carried head.
Skylark drooped as Maroon drew by,
Their hackles lifted, they scored to cry.

★   ★   ★

The fox knew well that, before they tore him,
They should try their speed on the downs before him.
There were three more miles to the Wan Dyke Hill,
But his heart was high that he beat them still.

The wind of the downland charmed his bones,
So off he went for the Sarsen Stones.

★   ★   ★

The moan of the three great firs in the wind
And the 'Ai' of the foxhounds died behind;
Wind-dapples followed the hill-wind's breath
On the Kill Down Gorge where the Danes found death.
Larks scattered up; the peewits feeding
Rose in a flock from the Kill Down Steeding.
The hare leaped up from her form and swerved
Swift left for the Starveall, harebell-turved.
On the wind-bare thorn some longtails prinking
Cried sweet as though wind-blown glass were chinking.
Behind came thudding and loud halloo,
Or a cry from hounds as they came to view.

★   ★   ★

The pure clean air came sweet to his lungs,
Till he thought foul scorn of those crying tongues.
In a three mile more he would reach the haven
In the Wan Dyke croaked on by the raven.
In a three mile more he would make his berth
On the hard cool floor of a Wan Dyke earth,
Too deep for spade, too curved for terrier,
With the pride of the race to make rest the merrier.
In a three mile more he would reach his dream,
So his game heart gulped and he put on steam.

★   ★   ★

Like a rocket shot to a ship ashore
The lean red bolt of his body tore,
Like a ripple of wind running swift on grass;
Like a shadow on wheat when a cloud blows past,
Like a turn at the buoy in a cutter sailing
When the bright green gleam lips white at the railing.

Like the April snake whipping back to sheath,
Like the gannets' hurtle on fish beneath,
Like a kestrel chasing, like a sickle reaping,
Like all things swooping, like all things sweeping,
Like a hound for stay, like a stag for swift,
With his shadow beside like spinning drift.

★ ★ ★

Past the gibbet-stock all stuck with nails,
Where they hanged in chains what had hung at jails,
Past Ashmundshowe where Ashmund sleeps,
And none but the tumbling peewit weeps,
Past Curlew Calling, the gaunt grey corner
Where the curlew comes as a summer mourner,
Past Blowbury Beacon, shaking his fleece,
Where all winds hurry and none brings peace;
Then down on the mile-long green decline,
Where the turf's like spring and the air's like wine,
Where the sweeping spurs of the downland spill
Into Wan Brook Valley and Wan Dyke Hill.

★ ★ ★

On he went with a galloping rally
Past Maesbury Clump for Wan Brook Valley.
The blood in his veins went romping high,
'Get on, on, on, to the earth or die.'
The air of the downs went purely past
Till he felt the glory of going fast,
Till the terror of death, though there indeed,
Was lulled for a while by his pride of speed.
He was romping away from hounds and hunt,
He had Wan Dyke Hill and his earth in front,
In a one mile more when his point was made
He would rest in safety from dog or spade;

Nose between paws he would hear the shout
Of the 'Gone to earth!' to the hounds without,
The whine of the hounds, and their cat-feet gadding,
Scratching the earth, and their breath pad-padding:
He would hear the horn call hounds away,
And rest in peace till another day.

★   ★   ★

In one mile more he would lie at rest,
So for one mile more he would go his best.
He reached the dip at the long droop's end
And he took what speed he had still to spend.

So down past Maesbury beech-clump grey
That would not be green till the end of May,
Past Arthur's Table, the white chalk boulder,
Where pasque flowers purple the down's grey shoulder,
Past Quichelm's Keeping, past Harry's Thorn,
To Thirty Acre all thin with corn.

★   ★   ★

As he raced the corn towards Wan Dyke Brook
The pack had view of the way he took;
Robin hallooed from the downland's crest,
He capped them on till they did their best.
The quarter-mile to the Wan Brook's brink
Was raced as quick as a man can think.

★   ★   ★

And here, as he ran to the huntsman's yelling,
The fox first felt that the pace was telling;
His body and lungs seemed all grown old,
His legs less certain, his heart less bold,
The hound-noise nearer, the hill-slope steeper,
The thud in the blood of his body deeper.

His pride in his speed, his joy in the race,
Were withered away, for what use was pace?
He had run his best, and the hounds ran better,
Then the going worsened, the earth was wetter.
Then his brush drooped down till it sometimes dragged,
And his fur felt sick and his chest was tagged
With taggles of mud, and his pads seemed lead,
It was well for him he'd an earth ahead.

Down he went to the brook and over,
Out of the corn and into the clover,
Over the slope that the Wan Brook drains,
Past Battle Tump where they earthed the Danes,
Then up the hill that the Wan Dyke rings
Where the Sarsen Stones stand grand like kings.

*   *   *

Seven Sarsens of granite grim,
As he ran them by they looked at him;
As he leaped the lip of their earthen paling
The hounds were gaining and he was failing.

*   *   *

He passed the Sarsens, he left the spur,
He pressed uphill to the blasted fir,
He slipped as he leaped the hedge; he slithered.
'He's mine,' thought Robin. 'He's done; he's dithered.'

*   *   *

At the second attempt he cleared the fence,
He turned half-right where the gorse was dense,
He was leading hounds by a furlong clear.
He was past his best, but his earth was near.
He ran up gorse to the spring of the ramp,
The steep green wall of the dead men's camp,

He sidled up it and scampered down
To the deep green ditch of the Dead Men's Town.

    ★ ★ ★

Within, as he reached that soft green turf,
The wind, blowing lonely, moaned like surf,
Desolate ramparts rose up steep
On either side, for the ghosts to keep.
He raced the trench, past the rabbit warren,
Close-grown with moss which the wind made barren;
He passed the spring where the rushes spread,
And there in the stones was his earth ahead.
One last short burst upon failing feet—
There life lay waiting, so sweet, so sweet,
Rest in a darkness, balm for aches.

    ★ ★ ★

The earth was stopped. It was barred with stakes.

    ★ ★ ★

With the hounds at head so close behind
He had to run as he changed his mind.
This earth, as he saw, was stopped, but still
There was one earth more on the Wan Dyke Hill—
A rabbit burrow a furlong on,
He could kennel there till the hounds were gone.
Though his death seemed near he did not blench,
He upped his brush and he ran the trench.

    ★ ★ ★

He ran the trench while the wind moaned treble,
Earth trickled down, there were falls of pebble.
Down in the valley of that dark gash
The wind-withered grasses looked like ash.
Trickles of stones and earth fell down
In that dark alley of Dead Men's Town.

A hawk arose from a fluff of feathers,
From a distant fold came a bleat of wethers.
He heard no noise from the hounds behind
But the hill-wind moaning like something blind.

   ★ ★ ★

He turned the bend in the hill, and there
Was his rabbit-hole with its mouth worn bare;
But there, with a gun tucked under his arm,
Was young Sid Kissop of Purlpit's Farm,
With a white hob ferret to drive the rabbit
Into a net which was set to nab it.
And young Jack Cole peered over the wall,
And loosed a pup with a 'Z'bite en, Saul!'
The terrier pup attacked with a will,
So the fox swerved right and away downhill.

   ★ ★ ★

Down from the ramp of the Dyke he ran
To the brackeny patch where the gorse began,
Into the gorse, where the hill's heave hid
The line he took from the eyes of Sid;
He swerved downwind and ran like a hare
For the wind-blown spinney below him there.

   ★ ★ ★

He slipped from the gorse to the spinney dark
(There were curled grey growths on the oak-tree bark);
He saw no more of the terrier pup,
But he heard men speak and the hounds come up.

   ★ ★ ★

He crossed the spinney with ears intent
For the cry of hounds on the way he went;
His heart was thumping, the hounds were near now,
He could make no sprint at a cry and cheer now,

He was past his perfect, his strength was failing,
His brush sag-sagged and his legs were ailing.
He felt, as he skirted Dead Men's Town,
That in one mile more they would have him down.

*   *   *

Through the withered oak's wind-crouching tops
He saw men's scarlet above the copse,
He heard men's oaths, yet he felt hounds slacken,
In the frondless stalks of the brittle bracken.
He felt that the unseen link which bound
His spine to the nose of the leading hound
Was snapped, that the hounds no longer knew
Which way to follow nor what to do;
That the threat of the hounds' teeth left his neck,
They had ceased to run, they had come to check.
They were quartering wide on the Wan Hill's bent.

*   *   *

The terrier's chase had killed his scent.

*   *   *

He heard bits chink as the horses shifted,
He heard hounds cast, then he heard hounds lifted,
But there came no cry from a new attack;
His heart grew steady, his breath came back.

*   *   *

He left the spinney and ran its edge
By the deep dry ditch of the blackthorn hedge;
Then out of the ditch and down the meadow,
Trotting at ease in the blackthorn shadow,
Over the track called Godsdown Road,
To the great grass heave of the gods' abode.
He was moving now upon land he knew:
Up Clench Royal and Morton Tew,

The Pol Brook, Cheddesdon, and East Stoke Church,
High Clench St Lawrence and Tinker's Birch.
Land he had roved on night by night,
For hot blood-suckage or furry bite.
The threat of the hounds behind was gone;
He breathed deep pleasure and trotted on.

While young Sid Kissop thrashed the pup
Robin on Pip came heaving up,
And found his pack spread out at check.
'I'd like to wring your terrier's neck,'
He said, 'you see? He's spoiled our sport.
He's killed the scent.' He broke off short,
And stared at hounds and at the valley.
No jay or magpie gave a rally
Down in the copse, no circling rooks
Rose over fields; old Joyful's looks
Were doubtful in the gorse, the pack
Quested both up and down and back.
He watched each hound for each small sign.
They tried, but could not hit the line,
The scent was gone. The field took place
Out of the way of hounds. The pace
Had tailed them out; though four remained;
Sir Peter, on White Rabbit, stained
Red from the brooks, Bill Ridden cheery,
Hugh Colway with his mare dead weary,
The Colonel with Marauder beat.
They turned towards a thud of feet;
Dansey, and then young Cothill came
(His chestnut mare was galloped tame).
'There's Copse a field behind,' he said.
'Those last miles put them all to bed.

They're strung along the downs like flies.'
Copse and Nob Manor topped the rise.
'Thank God! A check,' they said, 'at last.'

★   ★   ★

'They cannot own it; you must cast,'
Sir Peter said. The soft horn blew,
Tom turned the hounds upwind. They drew
Upwind, downhill, by spinney-side.
They tried the brambled ditch; they tried
The swamp, all choked with bright green grass
And clumps of rush, and pools like glass,
Long since the dead men's drinking pond.
They tried the white-leaved oak beyond,
But no hound spoke to it or feathered.
The horse-heads drooped like horses tethered,
The men mopped brows. 'An hour's hard run.
Ten miles,' they said, 'we must have done.
It's all of six from Colston's Gorses.'
The lucky got their second horses.

★   ★   ★

The time ticked by. 'He's lost,' they muttered.
A pheasant rose. A rabbit scuttered.
Men mopped their scarlet cheeks and drank.
They drew downwind along the bank
(The Wan Way) on the hill's south spur,
Grown with dwarf oak and juniper,
Like dwarves alive, but no hound spoke.
The seepings made the ground one soak.
They turned the spur; the hounds were beat.
Then Robin shifted in his seat
Watching for signs, but no signs showed.
'I'll lift across the Godsdown Road

D.—11

Beyond the spinney,' Robin said.
Tom turned them; Robin went ahead.

★   ★   ★

Beyond the copse a great grass fallow
Stretched towards Stoke and Cheddesdon Mallow,
A rolling grass where hounds grew keen.
'Yoi doit, then! This is where he's been,'
Said Robin, eager at their joy.
'Yooi, Joyful, lad! Yooi, Cornerboy!
They're on to him.'
      At his reminders
The keen hounds hurried to the finders.
The finding hounds began to hurry,
Men jammed their hats, prepared to scurry.
The 'Ai, Ai,' of the cry began,
Its spirit passed to horse and man;
The skirting hounds romped to the cry.
Hound after hound cried 'Ai, Ai, Ai,'
Till all were crying, running, closing,
Their heads well up and no heads nosing.
Joyful ahead with spear-straight stern
They raced the great slope to the burn.
Robin beside them, Tom behind
Pointing past Robin down the wind.

★   ★   ★

For there, two furlongs on, he viewed
On Holy Hill or Cheddesdon Rood,
Just where the ploughland joined the grass,
A speck down the first furrow pass,
A speck the colour of the plough.
'Yonder he goes. We'll have him now,'

He cried. The speck passed slowly on,
It reached the ditch, paused, and was gone.

*   *   *

Then down the slope and up the Rood
Went the hunt's gallop. Godsdown Wood
Dropped its last oak-leaves at the rally.
Over the Rood to High Clench Valley
The gallop led: the redcoats scattered,
The fragments of the hunt were tattered
Over five fields, ev'n since the check.
'A dead fox or a broken neck,'
Said Robin Dawe. 'Come up, the Dane.'
The hunter lent against the rein,
Cocking his ears; he loved to see
The hounds at cry. The hounds and he
The chiefs in all that feast of pace.

*   *   *

The speck in front began to race.

The fox heard hounds get on to his line,
And again the terror went down his spine;
Again the back of his neck felt cold,
From the sense of the hounds' teeth taking hold.
But his legs were rested, his heart was good,
He had breath to gallop to Mourne End Wood;
It was four miles more, but an earth at end,
So he put on pace down the Rood Hill Bend.

*   *   *

Down the great grass slope which the oak-trees dot,
With a swerve to the right from the keeper's cot,
Over High Clench Brook in its channel deep
To the grass beyond, where he ran to sheep.

*   *   *

The sheep formed line like a troop of horse,
They swerved, as he passed, to front his course.
From behind, as he ran, a cry arose:
'See the sheep there. Watch them. There he goes!'

*   *   *

He ran the sheep that their smell might check
The hounds from his scent and save his neck,
But in two fields more he was made aware
That the hounds still ran; Tom had viewed him there.

*   *   *

Tom had held them on through the taint of sheep;
They had kept his line, as they meant to keep.
They were running hard with a burning scent,
And Robin could see which way he went.
The pace that he went brought strain to breath,
He knew as he ran that the grass was death.

*   *   *

He ran the slope towards Morton Tew
That the heave of the hill might stop the view,
Then he doubled down to the Blood Brook red,
And swerved upstream in the brook's deep bed.
He splashed the shallows, he swam the deeps,
He crept by banks as a moorhen creeps;
He heard the hounds shoot over his line,
And go on, on, on, towards Cheddesdon Zine.

*   *   *

In the minute's peace he could slacken speed,
The ease from the strain was sweet indeed.
Cool to the pads the water flowed.
He reached the bridge on the Cheddesdon Road.

*   *   *

As he came to light from the culvert dim
Two boys on the bridge looked down on him;

They were young Bill Ripple and Harry Meun;
'Look, there be squirrel, a-swimmin', see 'un?'

'Noa, ben't a squirrel, be fox, be fox.
Now, Hal, get pebble, we'll give 'en socks.'
'Get pebble, Billy, dub 'un a plaster;
There's for thy belly, I'll learn 'ee, master.'

*   *   *

The stones splashed spray in the fox's eyes,
He raced from brook in a burst of shies,
He ran for the reeds in the withy car,
Where the dead flags shake and the wild-duck are.

*   *   *

He pushed through the reeds, which cracked at his passing,
To the High Clench Water, a grey pool glassing;
He heard Bill Ripple, in Cheddesdon Road,
Shout, 'This way, huntsmen, it's here he goed.'

*   *   *

Then 'Leu, Leu, Leu,' went the soft horn's laughter,
The hounds (they had checked) came romping after;
The clop of the hooves on the road was plain,
Then the crackle of reeds, then cries again.

*   *   *

A whimpering first, then Robin's cheer,
Then the 'Ai, Ai, Ai'; they were all too near,
His swerve had brought but a minute's rest;
Now he ran again, and he ran his best.

*   *   *

With a crackle of dead dry stalks of reed
The hounds came romping at topmost speed;
The redcoats ducked as the great hooves skittered
The Blood Brook's shallows to sheets that glittered;

With a cracking whip and a 'Hoik, Hoik, Hoik,
Forrard!' Tom galloped. Bob shouted 'Yoick!'
Like a running fire the dead reeds crackled;
The hounds' heads lifted, their necks were hackled.
Tom cried to Bob, as they thundered through,
'He is running short, we shall kill at Tew.'
Bob cried to Tom as they rode in team,
'I was sure, that time, that he turned upstream.
As the hounds went over the brook in stride
I saw old Daffodil fling to side,
So I guessed at once, when they checked beyond.'

      ★   ★   ★

The ducks flew up from the Morton Pond;
The fox looked up at their tailing strings,
He wished (perhaps) that a fox had wings.
Wings with his friends in a great V straining
The autumn sky when the moon is gaining;
For better the grey sky's solitude
Then to be two miles from the Mourne End Wood
With the hounds behind, clean-trained to run,
And your strength half spent and your breath half done.
Better the reeds and the sky and water
Than that hopeless pad from a certain slaughter.
At the Morton Pond the fields began—
Long Tew's green meadows; he ran, he ran.

      ★   ★   ★

First the six green fields that make a mile,
With the lip-ful Clench at the side the while,
With rooks above, slow-circling, showing
The world of men where a fox was going;
The fields all empty, dead grass, bare hedges,
And the brook's bright gleam in the dark of sedges.

To all things else he was dumb and blind;
He ran with the hounds a field behind.

* * *

At the sixth green field came the long slow climb
To the Mourne End Wood, as old as time;
Yew woods dark, where they cut for bows,
Oak woods green with the mistletoes,
Dark woods evil, but burrowed deep
With a brock's earth strong, where a fox might sleep.
He saw his point on the heaving hill,
He had failing flesh and a reeling will;
He felt the heave of the hill grow stiff,
He saw black woods, which would shelter—if
Nothing else, but the steepening slope
And a black line nodding, a line of hope—
The line of the yews on the long slope's brow,
A mile, three-quarters, a half-mile now.

* * *

A quarter-mile, but the hounds had viewed;
They yelled to have him this side the wood.
Robin capped them. Tom Dansey steered them;
With a 'Yooi! Yooi! Yooi!' Bill Ridden cheered them.
Then up went hackles as Shatterer led.
'Mob him!' cried Ridden, 'the wood's ahead.
Turn him, damn it! Yooi! beauties, beat him,
O God, let them get him: let them eat him!
O God!' said Ridden, 'I'll eat him stewed,
If you'll let us get him this side the wood.'

* * *

But the pace, uphill, made a horse like stone;
The pack went wild up the hill alone.

* * *

Three hundred yards and the worst was past,
The slope was gentler and shorter-grassed;
The fox saw the bulk of the woods grow tall
On the brae ahead, like a barrier-wall.
He saw the skeleton trees show sky
And the yew-trees darken to see him die,
And the line of the woods go reeling black:
There was hope in the woods—and behind, the pack.

*   *   *

Two hundred yards and the trees grew taller,
Blacker, blinder, as hope grew smaller;
Cry seemed nearer, the teeth seemed gripping,
Pulling him back; his pads seemed slipping.
He was all one ache, one gasp, one thirsting,
Heart on his chest-bones, beating, bursting;
The hounds were gaining like spotted pards,
And the wood hedge still was a hundred yards.

*   *   *

The wood hedge black was a two-year, quick
Cut-and-laid that had sprouted thick
Thorns all over and strongly plied.
With a clean red ditch on the take-off side.

*   *   *

He saw it now as a redness, topped
With a wattle of thorn-work spiky cropped,
Spiky to leap on, stiff to force,
No safe jump for a failing horse;
But beyond it darkness of yews together,
Dark green plumes over soft brown feather.
Darkness of woods where scents were blowing—
Strange scents, hot scents, of wild things going,
Scents that might draw these hounds away.

So he ran, ran, ran to that clean red clay.

*   *   *

Still, as he ran, his pads slipped back,
All his strength seemed to draw the pack,
The trees drew over him dark like Norns,
He was over the ditch and at the thorns.

*   *   *

He thrust at the thorns, which would not yield;
He leaped, but fell, in sight of the field.
The hounds went wild as they saw him fall,
The fence stood stiff like a Bucks flint wall.

*   *   *

He gathered himself for a new attempt;
His life before was an old dream dreamt,
All that he was was a blown fox quaking,
Jumping at thorns too stiff for breaking,
While over the grass in crowd, in cry,
Came the grip teeth grinning to make him die,
The eyes intense, dull, smouldering red,
The fell like a ruff round each keen head,
The pace like fire, and scarlet men
Galloping, yelling, 'Yooi, eat him, then!'

*   *   *

He gathered himself, he leaped, he reached
The top of the hedge like a fish-boat beached.
He steadied a second and then leaped down
To the dark of the wood where bright things drown.

*   *   *

He swerved, sharp right, under young green firs.
Robin called on the Dane with spurs.
He cried, 'Come, Dansey; if God's not good,
We shall change our fox in this Mourne End Wood.'

Tom cried back as he charged like spate,
'Mine can't jump that, I must ride to gate.'
Robin answered, 'I'm going at him.
I'll kill that fox, if it kills me, drat him!
We'll kill in covert. Gerr on, now, Dane.'
He gripped him tight and he made it plain,
He slowed him down till he almost stood,
While his hounds went crash into Mourne End Wood.

*   *   *

Like a dainty dancer, with footing nice
The Dane turned side for a leap in twice.
He cleared the ditch to the red clay bank,
He rose at the fence as his quarters sank,
He barged the fence as the bank gave way,
And down he came in a fall of clay.

*   *   *

Robin jumped off him and gasped for breath.
He said, 'That's lost him as sure as death.
They've overrun him. Come up, the Dane.
We'll kill him yet, if we ride to Spain.'

*   *   *

He scrambled up to his horse's back,
He thrust through cover, he called his pack;
He cheered them on till they made it good,
Where the fox had swerved inside the wood.

*   *   *

The fox knew well as he ran the dark,
That the headlong hounds were past their mark;
They had missed his swerve and had overrun,
But their devilish play was not yet done.

*   *   *

For a minute he ran and heard no sound,

Then a whimper came from a questing hound,
Then a 'This way, beauties,' and then 'Leu, Leu,'
The floating laugh of the horn that blew.
Then the cry again, and the crash and rattle
Of the shrubs burst back as they ran to battle,
Till the wood behind seemed risen from root,
Crying and crashing, to give pursuit,
Till the trees seemed hounds and the air seemed cry,
And the earth so far that he needs must die,
Die where he reeled in the woodland dim,
With a hound's white grips in the spine of him.
For one more burst he could spurt, and then
Wait for the teeth, and the wrench, and men.

*   *   *

He made his spurt for the Mourne End rocks
The air blew rank with the taint of fox;
The yews gave way to a greener space
Of great stone strewn in a grassy place.
And there was his earth at the great grey shoulder
Sunk in the ground, of a granite boulder.
A dry, deep burrow with rocky roof,
Proof against crowbars, terrier-proof,
Life to the dying, rest for bones.

*   *   *

The earth was stopped; it was filled with stones.

*   *   *

Then, for a moment, his courage failed,
His eyes looked up as his body quailed,
Then the coming of death, which all things dread,
Made him run for the wood ahead.

*   *   *

The taint of fox was rank on the air,
He knew, as he ran, there were foxes there.

His strength was broken, his heart was bursting,
His bones were rotten, his throat was thirsting;
His feet were reeling, his brush was thick
From dragging the mud, and his brain was sick.

*   *   *

He thought as he ran of his old delight
In the wood in the moon in an April night,
His happy hunting, his winter loving,
The smells of things in the midnight roving,
The look of his dainty-nosing, red,
Clean-felled dam with her footpad's tread;
Of his sire, so swift, so game, so cunning,
With craft in his brain and power of running;
Their fights of old when his teeth drew blood,
Now he was sick, with his coat all mud.

*   *   *

He crossed the covert, he crawled the bank,
To a meuse in the thorns, and there he sank,
With his ears flexed back and his teeth shown white,
In a rat's resolve for a dying bite.

*   *   *

And there, as he lay, he saw the vale,
That a struggling sunlight silvered pale:
The Deerlip Brook like a strip of steel,
The Nun's Wood Yews where the rabbits squeal,
The great grass square of the Roman Fort,
And the smoke in the elms at Crendon Court.

*   *   *

And above the smoke in the elm-tree tops
Was the beech-clump's blur, Blown Hilcote Copse,
Where he and his mates had long made merry
In the bloody joys of the rabbit-herry.

*   *   *

And there as he lay and looked, the cry
Of the hounds at head came rousing by;
He bent his bones in the blackthorn dim.

⋆　　　⋆　　　⋆

But the cry of the hounds was not for him.
Over the fence with a crash they went,
Belly to grass, with a burning scent;
Then came Dansey, yelling to Bob:
'They've changed! Oh, damn it! now here's a job.'
And Bob yelled back: 'Well, we cannot turn 'em,
It's Jumper and Antic, Tom, we'll learn 'em!
We must just go on, and I hope we kill.'
They followed hounds down the Mourne End Hill.

⋆　　　⋆　　　⋆

The fox lay still in the rabbit-meuse,
On the dry brown dust of the plumes of yews.
In the bottom below a brook went by,
Blue, in a patch, like a streak of sky.
There one by one, with a clink of stone,
Came a red or dark coat on a horse half-blown.
And man to man with a gasp for breath
Said: 'Lord, what a run! I'm fagged to death.'

⋆　　　⋆　　　⋆

After an hour no riders came,
The day drew by like an ending game;
A robin sang from a pufft red breast,
The fox lay quiet and took his rest.
A wren on a tree-stump carolled clear,
Then the starlings wheeled in a sudden sheer,
The rooks came home to the twiggy hive
In the elm-tree tops which the winds do drive.

Then the noise of the rooks fell slowly still,
And the lights came out in the Clench Brook Mill;
Then a pheasant cocked, then an owl began,
With the cry that curdles the blood of man.

*   *   *

The stars grew bright as the yews grew black,
The fox rose stiffly and stretched his back.
He flaired the air, then he padded out
To the valley below him, dark as doubt,
Winter-thin with the young green crops,
For old Cold Crendon and Hilcote Copse.

*   *   *

As he crossed the meadows at Naunton Larking
The dogs in the town all started barking,
For with feet all bloody and flanks all foam,
The hounds and the hunt were limping home;
Limping home in the dark dead-beaten,
The hounds all rank from a fox they'd eaten.
Dansey saying to Robin Dawe:
'The fastest and longest I ever saw.'
And Robin answered: 'Oh, Tom, 'twas good!
I thought they'd changed in the Mourne End Wood,
But now I feel that they did not change.
We've had a run that was great and strange;
And to kill in the end, at dusk, on grass!
We'll turn to the Cock and take a glass,
For the hounds, poor souls! are past their forces;
And a gallon of ale for our poor horses,
And some bits of bread for the hounds, poor things!
After all they've done (for they've done like kings)
Would keep them going till we get in.
We had it alone from Nun's Wood Whin.'

Then Tom replied: 'If they changed or not,
There've been few runs longer and none more hot,
We shall talk of to-day until we die.'

      ★   ★   ★

The stars grew bright in the winter sky,
The wind came keen with a tang of frost,
The brook was troubled for new things lost,
The copse was happy for old things found,
The fox came home and he went to ground.

      ★   ★   ★

And the hunt came home and the hounds were fed,
They climbed to their bench and went to bed;
The horses in stable loved their straw.
'Good-night, my beauties,' said Robin Dawe.

      ★   ★   ★

Then the moon came quiet and flooded full
Light and beauty on clouds like wool,
On a feasted fox at rest from hunting,
In the beech-wood grey where the brocks were grunting

      ★   ★   ★

The beech-wood grey rose dim in the night
With moonlight fallen in pools of light,
The long dead leaves on the ground were rimed;
A clock struck twelve and the church-bells chimed.